PUSHKIN PRESS CLASSICS

OUT OF
CHAOS
COMES
BLISS

'His poetry leaves echoes in the mind as music does, as all true poetry should… The whole man, body and mind, and the whole life are in the words. We see ourselves on the page, feel the arrow in the heart'

GUARDIAN

OUT OF CHAOS COMES BLISS

DYLAN THOMAS

SELECTED AND INTRODUCED
BY CERYS MATTHEWS

PUSHKIN PRESS CLASSICS

Pushkin Press
Somerset House, Strand
London WC2R ILA

Out of Chaos Comes Bliss was first published by Pushkin Press in 2024.

1 3 5 7 9 8 6 4 2

ISBN 13: 978-1-80533-119-3

Designed and typeset by Tetragon, London
Printed and bound in the United Kingdom by Clays Ltd, Elcograf S.p.A.

www.pushkinpress.com

CONTENTS

FROM *IN COUNTRY SLEEP* (1952)

LAST POEMS

A FINAL PRAYER

INTRODUCTION
I'd be a damn fool if I didn't!

I read somewhere of a shepherd who, when asked why he
made, from within fairy rings, ritual observances to the moon
to protect his flocks, replied: 'I'd be a damn fool if I didn't!'
These poems, with all their crudities, doubts, and confusions,
are written for the love of Man and in praise of God, and I'd
be a damn fool if they weren't

(DT, November 1952, in a Note to his *Collected Poems*)

And 'I'd be a damn fool if I didn't!' pretty much summed up
my reaction when Pushkin Press asked me to pull this book
together. Worm into the apple of his works and bring up a new
collection—for the suns of 2024? YES! With bells on.

Enter another quote from DT (throughout, as you've prob-
ably guessed, Dylan Thomas will be referred to as DT) to offer
up my freewheeling selection process:

Read the poems you like reading. Don't bother whether
they're important, or if they'll live. What does it matter
what poetry is, after all? If you want the definition of poetry,
say poetry IS what makes me laugh, or cry or yawn, what

makes my toenails twinkle, what makes me do this or that
or nothing and let it go with that.

(DT, in response to a question asked by a
University of Texas student in 1950)

So here we have them, poems which make toenails twinkle,
make you laugh or cry, which sing the loudest, have the most
unforgettable imagery, lines, the best stories, are most revealing
about the world then or now—or about the man, and boy,
who held the pen.

Many of these poems were written by DT while he was still
a teenager. I was curious to see just how early you can trace this
precociousness. With excitement, I include several examples
of 'unpublishable' juvenilia never before published together,
including his first nationally published poems, first for Wales
only, and then his first issued UK-wide.

For further interest about his family and the early years,
here is an extract of a conversation between my uncle Colin
Edwards and DT's mother Florence in 1958:

'He must have been a very bright child.'

'Oh, he was. And then, whenever it was wet or any-
thing, you had no trouble in entertaining him. Give him
plenty of notepaper or pencils, he'd go into his own little
bedroom and write and write and write. And reams of
poems.'

'At what age did this start?'

'Oh, he started about eight, I should think. And he'd ask
his sister, Nancy, sometimes, "What shall I write about now?"

And you know what sisters are, they're not very patient with their brothers, and she'd say, "Oh, write about the kitchen sink!" He wrote a poem, a most interesting little poem, about the kitchen sink. Then about an onion.'

(From *Dylan Remembered: Vol I, 1914–1934*, ed. David N. Thomas)

You'll find more from this conversation, as well as other quotes and notes about the poems, at the back of this book, though I'm not sure DT would approve of these, either: he was the one who called the juvenilia 'unpublishable'.

He would most probably rather we let the poems talk for themselves, and for us to take them literally, draw a breath and jump in with

'I AM GOING TO READ ALOUD.'

And off you'd go reading.

But that's him, and this is my tribute to him, and he's not here, alas, to fight. Besides, I'd like to imagine that he'd rather enjoy the ride in a way. As for the endnotes, I've included quotes from DT regarding specific poems as often as I thought worked.

Now, back to the reciting:

Then the man rose and rhythmically swaying on the ball of his feet... he let loose the wanton power of his voice... It made us yield to his spell... words were full of witchery.

(Professor Cecil Price, head of English at Swansea University, who invited DT to speak to students in April 1951)

11

I don't remember quite when I was bedevilled by his words. I grew up with the same view of the crescent-shaped bay in Swansea, but we never studied DT's writing at school.

My uncle Colin, mentioned above, amassed hundreds of hours of taped interviews in the 1950s and 1960s with DT's closest family, friends and associates (grist to the mill for many a subsequent book and article by academics), but I was too young or foolish to make the most of that connection.

It wasn't until I was away from Wales, in South Carolina, pregnant with my first child, when I happened on a tiny tree-ornament book of DT's, *A Child's Christmas in Wales* (first published 1950):

'Our snow was not only shaken from whitewash buckets down the sky, it came shawling out of the ground and swam and drifted out of the arms and hands and bodies of the trees; snow grew overnight on the roofs of the houses like a pure and grandfather moss, minutely ivied the walls and settled on the postman, opening the gate, like a dumb, numb thunderstorm of white, torn Christmas cards.'

'Were there postmen then, too?'

'With sprinkling eyes and wind-cherried noses, on spread, frozen feet they crunched up to the doors and mittened on them manfully. But all that the children could hear was a ringing of bells.'

'You mean that the postman went rat-a-tat-tat and the doors rang?'

'I mean that the bells the children could hear were inside them.'

I was smitten, the tender writing seen above, the humour, heart and cheek—lines like 'Ernie Jenkins, he loves fires', 'an aunt now, alas, no longer whinnying with us', and scenes of chaos played out in homes across Christmas:

> Auntie Bessie, who had already been frightened, twice, by a clock-work mouse, whimpered at the sideboard and had some elderberry wine. The dog was sick. Auntie Dosie had to have three aspirins, but Auntie Hannah, who liked port, stood in the middle of the snowbound back yard, singing like a big-bosomed thrush.

Roll on twenty years and DT has become a massive part of my life—I've got a musical of *A Child's Christmas* running in Minneapolis for its second year, an illustrated children's edition of *Under Milk Wood* (1954) with artist Kate Evans, a ballet choreographed around his poems and I have written and presented many documentaries with DT at their heart.

But let's go back to him then, and Professor Cecil Price again: 'His poetry was an incantation, a charm to rob evil and good of their influences and leave us all naked things of sense.' Which means job done for DT. Here he is answering the question 'Have you been influenced by Freud and how do you regard him?':

> Yes. Whatever is hidden should be made naked. To be stripped of darkness is to be clean, to strip of darkness is to make clean. Poetry, recording the stripping of the individual darkness, must inevitably cast light upon what has

13

been hidden for too long, and by so doing, make clean the naked exposure.

(From 'Answers to an Enquiry', first published in *New Verse*, 11th October 1934)

But why did DT start writing poetry in the first place? Again, here he is:

I should say I wanted to write poetry in the beginning because I had fallen in love with words. The first poems I knew were nursery rhymes, and before I could read them for myself I had come to love just the words of them, the words alone… There they were, seemingly lifeless, made only of black and white, but out of them, out of their own being, came love and terror and pity and pain and wonder and all the other vague abstractions that make our ephemeral lives dangerous, great, and bearable.

(From 'Poetic Manifesto', first published in *Texas Quarterly*, 1961)

Let me take you back to 2009. I'm now in one of the front-row terraced houses that line the Mumbles Road with Gwen Watkins, writer and widow of poet Vernon Watkins and DT's friend, who was telling me about this very thing: the young Dylan was in love with the sounds of words, especially 'Ride a cock-horse to Banbury Cross'. Remember it? It goes like this:

Ride a cock-horse to Banbury Cross,
To see a fine lady upon a white horse;

Rings on her fingers and bells on her toes,
And she shall have music wherever she goes.

That line—'And she shall have music wherever she goes'—
could well be describing DT's wordplay: he took the English
language and made it sing.

It's now 2023, I'm mildly hungover on a very wet August
Saturday and reading in the window, watching the River
Thames:

Under the mile off moon we trembled listening
To the sea sound flowing like blood from the loud wound
And when the salt sheet broke in a storm of singing
The voices of all the drowned swam on the wind.

(From 'Lie still, sleep becalmed')

As in the song 'Wichita Lineman', we hear Dylan Thomas
humming through the lines… singing in the wires.

We're here with him now—the sounds he conjures—and
I am taken back to chapel, where we'd go three times on a
Sunday, bathed by the warm heart of hymns—seducing—and
bookended with more storytelling, this time from the pulpit,
and another familiar sound, the dynamics and drama, ebb and
flow of a sermon.

On he goes in 'Lie still, sleep becalmed':

We heard the sea sound sing, we saw the salt sheet tell.
Lie still, sleep becalmed, hide the mouth in the throat,
Or we shall obey, and ride with you through the drowned.

The world of Dylan Thomas is a giving one. Once you connect with his writing, be it from a play, an essay, story or poem, his words never leave you. Favourite lines or images find homes in the nooks and crannies of your mind, and, once in a while, pop out:

'What'll the neighbours…?'
'Though I sang in my chains like the sea'
'Fishingboatbobbing sea'
'Do not go gentle'
'And death shall have no dominion'
'Books that told me everything about the wasp, except why'
'Got off the bus, and forgot to get on again'
'Yes, Mog, Yes'

And the line which gave this book its title— 'out of the chaos would come bliss'—from his poem 'Being but men, we walked into the trees'.

Like every great artist, his style reads as effortless, though he often acknowledged the labour behind the magic:

What I like to do is to treat words as a craftsman does his wood or stone or what-have-you, to hew, carve, mould, coil, polish and plane them into patterns, sequences, sculptures, fugues of sound expressing some lyrical impulse, some spiritual doubt or conviction, some dimly realised truth I must try to reach and realise.

('Poetic Manifesto')

His delight in the malleability and sound of language, his understanding across both Welsh[*] and English, and knowledge of Auden, Donne, Joyce, Blake, Keats, Shakespeare, Wilfred Owen, among others, come together and make his work striking and original.

He'd have been familiar with the Welsh-language Bible, Welsh-language chapel services (he too went three times on a Sunday) and also the *Mabinogion*, a collection of stories passed on orally then written down in the twelfth and thirteenth centuries. These were presented in Middle Welsh—largely understandable to the modern Welsh speaker. Dylan was even named after one of the characters, Dylan ail Don (Dylan, second wave) from 'Math fab Mathonwy'.

On this note, the name was used very rarely—hard to imagine now, it being so popular across the Atlantic too, in whichever spelling...

Another note to add: Dylan, in Thomas's case, must rhyme with villain, according to his mam, Florrie. This is not the conventional Welsh way: conventionally Dylan would sound like Dull-Anne, with emphasis on the dull.

Back to my book, which I hope you're not finding dull so far. Why am I presenting this in 2024? And why poetry? Again I turn to DT to see what he says on the matter; did he intend his poetry to be useful?

---

[*]   Although there's no recording of DT speaking Welsh, there's no way he didn't understand it. Back in the 1910s, 1920s and 1930s it would have been the predominant language used by the farming communities of Carmarthen and West Wales, where he spent so much of his childhood. More on that in the endnotes.

My poetry is, or should be, useful to me for one reason: it is the record of my individual struggle from darkness towards some measure of light… My poetry is, or should be, useful to others for its individual recording of that same struggle with which they are necessarily acquainted.

('Answers to an Enquiry')

Here's DT again, from his essay 'On Poetry' in *Quite Early One Morning* (1945):

A good poem is a contribution to reality. The world is never the same once a good poem has been added to it. A good poem helps to change the shape and significance of the universe, helps to extend everyone's knowledge of himself and the world around him.

With these lofty ambitions in mind, this is probably a good place and time to end my ramblings and instead let me welcome the poems themselves to take centre stage.

I hope you enjoy.

I hope too that you'll find the magic in them there syllables…

CERYS MATTHEWS

(VERY) EARLY POEMS

The Song of the Mischievous Dog

There are many who say that a dog has its day,
    And a cat has a number of lives;
There are others who think that a lobster is pink,
    And that bees never work in their hives.
There are fewer, of course, who insist that a horse
    Has a horn and two humps on its head,
And a fellow who jests that a mare can build nests
    Is as rare as a donkey that's red.
Yet in spite of all this, I have moments of bliss,
    For I cherish a passion for bones,
And though doubtful of biscuit, I'm willing to risk it,
    And love to chase rabbits and stones.
But my greatest delight is to take a good bite
    At a calf that is plump and delicious;
And if I indulge in a bite at a bulge,
    Let's hope you won't think me too vicious.

'The Second Best'

You ask me for a toast to-night
    In this familiar hall,
Where well-known objects greet the sight,
    And boyhood's days recall.

'Some honoured name,' I think you said,
    But what have I to say?
The King, the Services, the Head,
    The heroes of the day—

To each with joyous shouts and pride
    Has loud acclaim been paid;
Forgive me, if I turn aside
    From sunshine into shade.

For now a shadow-throng I see,
    From seats long vacant rise,
A faint reproach there seems to be
    In their world-weary eyes.

Their voices cross our song and jest
    From camp and field and town—
The men who did their level best,
    Yet never won renown.

Amongst the nameless dead they lie
    In unrecorded graves;
And o'er their memory roll high
    The world's oblivious waves,

Yet though the school they loved so well
    No more records their name,
Though on their brows there may not dwell
    A crown of earthly fame,

Though on life's battlefield their part
    Was not to gain the prize,
Still deep in some old comrade's heart
    Enshrined their memory lies.

I give to-night no foremost name,
    I give no honoured guest;
I think of those unknown to fame,
    I give 'The Second Best.'

La Danseuse

She moved like silence swathed in light,
Like mist in moonshine clear;
A music that enamoured sight
Yet did elude the ear.

A rapture and a spirit clad
In motion soft as sleep;
The epitome of all things glad,
The sum of all that weep.

Her form was like a poet's mind,
By all sensations sought.
She seemed the substance of the wind,
One shape of lyric thought;

A being 'mid terrestrial things
Transcendently forlorn;
Through time bound far on gleaming wings
For some diviner bourn.

The rhythms of the swooning heart
Swayed to her sweet control;
Life in her keeping all was art,
And all of body soul.

Faint-shimmering in the roseate air
She seemed to ebb and flow
Like memories perilously fair,
And pale from long ago.

Forest Picture

Calm and strange is this evening hour in the forest,
Carven domes of green are the trees by the pathway,
Infinite shadowy isles lie silent before me,
Summer is heavy with age, and leans upon Autumn.

All the land is ripe. There is no motion
Down the long bays of blue that those cloudy headlands
Sleep above in the glow of a fading sunset;
All things rest in the will of purpose triumphant.

Outlines melting into a vague immensity
Fade, the green gloom grows darker, and deeper the dusk:
Hark! a voice and laughter—the living and loving
Down these fantastic avenues pass like shadows.

Clown in the Moon

My tears are like the quiet drift
Of petals from some magic rose;
And all my grief flows from the rift
Of unremembered skies and snows.

I think, that if I touched the earth,
    It would crumble;
It is so sad and beautiful,
So tremulously like a dream.

The Pine

Virgate and sprung of the dusk,
The pine is the tree of the breeze,
And the winds that stream through the ribboned light
And the motley winds from the seas.

No, pigeon, I'm too wise

No, pigeon, I'm too wise;
No sky for me that carries
Its shining clouds for you;
Sky has not loved me much,
And if it did, who should I have
To wing my shoulders and my feet?
There's no way.
Ah, nightingale, my voice
Could never touch your spinning notes,
Nor be so clear.
I'm not secure enough
To tell what note I could reach if I tried,
But no high tree for me
With branches waiting for a singing bird,
And every nightingale a swan
Who sails on tides of leaves and sound.
I'm all for ground,
To touch what's to be touched,
To imitate myself mechanically,
Doing my little tricks of speech again
With all my usual care.
No bird for me:
He flies too high.

NOTEBOOK POEMS

Cabaret
(or I, poor romantic, held her heel)

I, poor romantic, held her heel
Upon the island of my palm,
And saw towards her tiny face
Going her glistening calves that minute.
There was a purpose in her pointed foot;
Her thighs and underclothes were sweet,
And drew my spiral breath
To circumambulate for decency
Their golden and their other colour.
The band was playing on the balcony.
One lady's hand was lifted,
But she did not cry, 'I see;
I see the man is mad with love.'
Her fan burst in a million lights
As that her heel was lifted,
Gone from my palm to leave it marked
With quite a kind of heart.
She is on dancing toes again,
Sparkling a twelve-legged body
And many arms to raise
Over her heel and me.
I, poor romantic, contemplate
The insect on this painted tree.
Which is the metal wing
And which the real?

Being but men, we walked into the trees

Being but men, we walked into the trees
Afraid, letting our syllables be soft
For fear of waking the rooks,
For fear of coming
Noiselessly into a world of wings and cries.

If we were children we might climb,
Catch the rooks sleeping, and break no twig,
And, after the soft ascent,
Thrust out our heads above the branches
To wonder at the unfailing stars.

Out of confusion, as the way is,
And the wonder that man knows,
Out of the chaos would come bliss.

That, then, is loveliness, we said,
Children in wonder watching the stars,
Is the aim and the end.

Being but men, we walked into the trees.

Before the gas fades

Before the gas fades with a harsh last bubble,
And the hunt in the hatstand discovers no coppers,
Before the last fag and the shirt sleeves and slippers,
The century's trap will have snapped round your middle,
Before the allotment is weeded and sown,
And the oakum is picked, and the spring trees have grown green,
And the state falls to bits,
And is fed to the cats,
Before civilisation rises or rots
(It's a matter of guts,
Graft, poison, and bluff,
Sobstuff, mock reason,
The chameleon coats of the big bugs and shots),
The jaws will have shut, and life be switched out.
Before the arrival of angel or devil,
Before evil or good, light or dark,
Before white or black, the right or left sock,
Before good or bad luck.

Man's manmade sparetime lasts the four seasons,
Is empty in springtime, and no other time lessens
The bitter, the wicked, the longlying leisure,
Sleep punctured by waking, dreams
Broken by choking,
The hunger of living, the oven and gun
That turned on and lifted in anger
Make the hunger for living

When the purse is empty
And the belly is empty,
The harder to bear and the stronger.
The century's trap will have closed for good
About you, flesh will perish, and blood
Run down the world's gutters,
Before the world steadies, stop rocking, is steady,
Or rocks, swings and rocks, before the world totters.

Caught in the trap's machinery, lights out,
With sightless eyes and hearts that do not beat,
You will not see the steadying or falling,
Under the heavy layers of the night
Not black or white or left or right.

'We who were young are old'

'We who were young are old. It is the oldest cry.
Age sours before youth's tasted in the mouth
And any sweetness that it has
Is sucked away.'

We who are still young are old. It is a dead cry,
The squeal of the damned out of the old pit.
We have grown weak before we could grow strong,
For us there is no shooting and no riding,
The Western man has lost one lung
And cannot mount a clotheshorse without bleeding.

Until the whisper of the last trump louden
We shall play Chopin in our summer garden,
With half-averted heads, as if to listen,
Play Patience in the parlour after dark.
For us there is no riding and no shooting,
No frosty gallops through the winter park.
We who are young sit holding yellow hands
Before the fire, and hearken to the wind.

No faith to fix the teeth on carries
Men old before their time into dark valleys
Where death lies dead asleep, one bright eye open,
No faith to sharpen the old wits leaves us
Lost in the shades, no course, no use
To fight through the invisible weeds,
No faith to follow is the world's curse
That falls on chaos.

There is but one message for the earth,
Young men with fallen chests and old men's breath,
Women with cancer at their sides
And cancerous speaking dripping from their mouths,
And lovers turning on the gas,
Ex-soldiers with horrors for a face,
A pig's snout for a nose,
The lost in doubt, the nearly mad, the young
Who, undeserving, have suffered the earth's wrong,
The living dead left over from the war,
The living after, the filled with fear,
The caught in the cage, the broken winged,
The flying loose, albino eyed, wing singed,
The white, the black, the yellow and mulatto
From Harlem, Bedlam, Babel, and the Ghetto,
The Piccadilly men, the back street drunks,
The grafters of cats' heads on chickens' trunks,
The whole, the crippled, the weak and strong,
The Western man with one lung gone—
Faith fixed beyond the spinning stars,
Fixed faith, believing and worshipping together
In god or gods, Christ or his father,
Mary, virgin, or any other.
Faith. Faith. Firm faith in many or one,
Faith fixed like a star beyond the stars,
And the skysigns and the night lights,
And the shores of the last sun.

We who are young are old, and unbelieving,
Sit at our hearths from morning until evening,
Warming dry hands and listening to the air;
We have no faith to set between our teeth.
Believe, believe and be saved, we cry, who have no faith.

Out of a war of wits

Out of a war of wits, when folly of words
Was the world's to me, and syllables
Fell hard as whips on an old wound,
My brain came crying into the fresh light,
Called for confessor but there was none
To purge after the wits' fight,
And I was struck dumb by the sun.
Praise that my body be whole, I've limbs
Not stumps, after the hour of battle,
For the body's brittle and the skin's white.
Praise that only the wits are hurt after the wits' fight.
The sun shines strong, dispels
Where men are men men's smells.
Overwhelmed by the sun, with a torn brain
I stand beneath the clouds' confessional,
But the hot beams rob me of speech,
After the perils of fools' talk
Reach asking arms up to the milky sky,
After a volley of questions and replies
Lift wit-hurt head for sun to sympathize,
And the sun heals, closing sore eyes.
It is good that the sun shine,
And, after it has sunk, the sane moon,
For out of a house of matchboard and stone
Where men would argue till the stars be green,
It is good to step onto the earth, alone,
And be struck dumb, if only for a time.

That sanity be kept

That sanity be kept I sit at open windows,
Regard the sky, make unobtrusive comment on the moon,
Sit at open windows in my shirt,
And let the traffic pass, the signals shine,
The engines run, the brass bands keep in tune,
For sanity must be preserved.

Thinking of death, I sit and watch the park
Where children play in all their innocence,
And matrons, on the littered grass,
Absorb the daily sun.

The sweet suburban music from a hundred lawns
Comes softly to my ears. The English mowers mow and mow.

I mark the couples walking arm in arm,
Observe their smiles,
Sweet invitations and inventions,
See them lend love illustration
By gesture and grimace.
I watch them curiously, detect beneath the laughs
What stands for grief, a vague bewilderment
At things not turning right.

I sit at open windows in my shirt,
Observe, like some Jehovah of the west,
What passes by, that sanity be kept.

For as long as forever is

For as long as forever is
And the fast sky quakes in the web, as the fox in the wave,
With heels of birds and the plumed eyes,
Shakes in its stride the partridge fence and the sea-duck rows,
And a flame in a wheel jumps the nave,
As a dozen winds drop the dark by the one moonrise,
And the stag through a trap grave,
Forever the hunted world at a snail's gallop goes.

Over the packed nests now, the snare and the she-bear's floes,
Through the cat's mountain and the cave
By the market and a feather street near the townspires,
Narrowly time's slow riders shave.

FROM
18 POEMS
(1934)

I see the boys of summer

I

I see the boys of summer in their ruin
Lay the gold tithings barren,
Setting no store by harvest, freeze the soils;
There in their heat the winter floods
Of frozen loves they fetch their girls,
And drown the cargoed apples in their tides.

These boys of light are curdlers in their folly,
Sour the boiling honey;
The jacks of frost they finger in the hives;
There in the sun the frigid threads
Of doubt and dark they feed their nerves;
The signal moon is zero in their voids.

I see the summer children in their mothers
Split up the brawned womb's weathers,
Divide the night and day with fairy thumbs;
There in the deep with quartered shades
Of sun and moon they paint their dams
As sunlight paints the shelling of their heads.

I see that from these boys shall men of nothing
Stature by seedy shifting,
Or lame the air with leaping from its heats;

There from their hearts the dogdayed pulse
Of love and light bursts in their throats.
O see the pulse of summer in the ice.

II

But seasons must be challenged or they totter
Into a chiming quarter
Where, punctual as death, we ring the stars;
There, in his night, the black-tongued bells
The sleepy man of winter pulls,
Nor blows back moon-and-midnight as she blows.

We are the dark deniers, let us summon
Death from a summer woman,
A muscling life from lovers in their cramp,
From the fair dead who flush the sea
The bright-eyed worm on Davy's lamp,
And from the planted womb the man of straw.

We summer boys in this four-winded spinning,
Green of the seaweeds' iron,
Hold up the noisy sea and drop her birds,
Pick the world's ball of wave and froth
To choke the deserts with her tides,
And comb the county gardens for a wreath.

In spring we cross our foreheads with the holly,
Heigh ho the blood and berry,
And nail the merry squires to the trees;

Here love's damp muscle dries and dies,
Here break a kiss in no love's quarry.
O see the poles of promise in the boys.

III

I see you boys of summer in your ruin.
Man in his maggot's barren.
And boys are full and foreign in the pouch.
I am the man your father was.
We are the sons of flint and pitch.
O see the poles are kissing as they cross.

The force that through the green fuse

The force that through the green fuse drives the flower
Drives my green age; that blasts the roots of trees
Is my destroyer.
And I am dumb to tell the crooked rose
My youth is bent by the same wintry fever.

The force that drives the water through the rocks
Drives my red blood; that dries the mouthing streams
Turns mine to wax.
And I am dumb to mouth unto my veins
How at the mountain spring the same mouth sucks.

The hand that whirls the water in the pool
Stirs the quicksand; that ropes the blowing wind
Hauls my shroud sail.
And I am dumb to tell the hanging man
How of my clay is made the hangman's lime.

The lips of time leech to the fountain head;
Love drips and gathers, but the fallen blood
Shall calm her sores.
And I am dumb to tell a weather's wind
How time has ticked a heaven round the stars.

And I am dumb to tell the lover's tomb
How at my sheet goes the same crooked worm.

Where once the waters of your face

Where once the waters of your face
Spun to my screws, your dry ghost blows,
The dead turns up its eye;
Where once the mermen through your ice
Pushed up their hair, the dry wind steers
Through salt and root and roe.

Where once your green knots sank their splice
Into the tided cord, there goes
The green unraveller,
His scissors oiled, his knife hung loose
To cut the channels at their source
And lay the wet fruits low.

Invisible, your clocking tides
Break on the lovebeds of the weeds;
The weed of love's left dry;
There round about your stones the shades
Of children go who, from their voids,
Cry to the dolphined sea.

Dry as a tomb, your coloured lids
Shall not be latched while magic glides
Sage on the earth and sky;
There shall be corals in your beds,
There shall be serpents in your tides,
Till all our sea-faiths die.

Especially when the October wind

Especially when the October wind
With frosty fingers punishes my hair,
Caught by the crabbing sun I walk on fire
And cast a shadow crab upon the land,
By the sea's side, hearing the noise of birds,
Hearing the raven cough in winter sticks,
My busy heart who shudders as she talks
Sheds the syllabic blood and drains her words.

Shut, too, in a tower of words, I mark
On the horizon walking like the trees
The wordy shapes of women, and the rows
Of the star-gestured children in the park.
Some let me make you of the vowelled beeches,
Some of the oaken voices, from the roots
Of many a thorny shire tell you notes,
Some let me make you of the water's speeches.

Behind a pot of ferns the wagging clock
Tells me the hour's word, the neural meaning
Flies on the shafted disk, declaims the morning
And tells the windy weather in the cock.
Some let me make you of the meadow's signs;
The signal grass that tells me all I know
Breaks with the wormy winter through the eye.
Some let me tell you of the raven's sins.

Especially when the October wind
(Some let me make you of autumnal spells,
The spider-tongued, and the loud hill of Wales)
With fist of turnips punishes the land,
Some let me make you of the heartless words.
The heart is drained that, spelling in the scurry
Of chemic blood, warned of the coming fury.
By the sea's side hear the dark-vowelled birds.

Light breaks where no sun shines

Light breaks where no sun shines;
Where no sea runs, the waters of the heart
Push in their tides;
And, broken ghosts with glow-worms in their heads,
The things of light
File through the flesh where no flesh decks the bones.

A candle in the thighs
Warms youth and seed and burns the seeds of age;
Where no seed stirs,
The fruit of man unwrinkles in the stars,
Bright as a fig;
Where no wax is, the candle shows its hairs.

Dawn breaks behind the eyes;
From poles of skull and toe the windy blood
Slides like a sea;
Nor fenced, nor staked, the gushers of the sky
Spout to the rod
Divining in a smile the oil of tears.

Night in the sockets rounds,
Like some pitch moon, the limit of the globes;
Day lights the bone;
Where no cold is, the skinning gales unpin
The winter's robes;
The film of spring is hanging from the lids.

Light breaks on secret lots,
On tips of thought where thoughts smell in the rain;
When logics die,
The secret of the soil grows through the eye,
And blood jumps in the sun;
Above the waste allotments the dawn halts.

I dreamed my genesis

I dreamed my genesis in sweat of sleep, breaking
Through the rotating shell, strong
As motor muscle on the drill, driving
Through vision and the girdered nerve.

From limbs that had the measure of the worm, shuffled
Off from the creasing flesh, filed
Through all the irons in the grass, metal
Of suns in the man-melting night.

Heir to the scalding veins that hold love's drop, costly
A creature in my bones I
Rounded my globe of heritage, journey
In bottom gear through night-geared man.

I dreamed my genesis and died again, shrapnel
Rammed in the marching heart, hole
In the stitched wound and clotted wind, muzzled
Death on the mouth that ate the gas.

Sharp in my second death I marked the hills, harvest
Of hemlock and the blades, rust
My blood upon the tempered dead, forcing
My second struggling from the grass.

And power was contagious in my birth, second
Rise of the skeleton and
Rerobing of the naked ghost. Manhood
Spat up from the resuffered pain.

I dreamed my genesis in sweat of death, fallen
Twice in the feeding sea, grown
Stale of Adam's brine until, vision
Of new man strength, I seek the sun.

FROM
TWENTY-FIVE POEMS
(1936)

Why east wind chills

Why east wind chills and south wind cools
Shall not be known till windwell dries
And west's no longer drowned
In winds that bring the fruit and rind
Of many a hundred falls;
Why silk is soft and the stone wounds
The child shall question all his days,
Why night-time rain and the breast's blood
Both quench his thirst he'll have a black reply.

When cometh Jack Frost? the children ask.
Shall they clasp a comet in their fists?
Not till, from high and low, their dust
Sprinkles in children's eyes a long-last sleep
And dusk is crowded with the children's ghosts,
Shall a white answer echo from the rooftops.

All things are known: the stars' advice
Calls some content to travel with the winds,
Though what the stars ask as they round
Time upon time the towers of the skies
Is heard but little till the stars go out.
I hear content, and 'Be content'
Ring like a handbell through the corridors,
And 'Know no answer,' and I know
No answer to the children's cry
Of echo's answer and the man of frost
And ghostly comets over the raised fists.

The hand that signed the paper

The hand that signed the paper felled a city;
Five sovereign fingers taxed the breath,
Doubled the globe of dead and halved a country;
These five kings did a king to death.

The mighty hand leads to a sloping shoulder,
The finger joints are cramped with chalk;
A goose's quill has put an end to murder
That put an end to talk.

The hand that signed the treaty bred a fever,
And famine grew, and locusts came;
Great is the hand that holds dominion over
Man by a scribbled name.

The five kings count the dead but do not soften
The crusted wound nor stroke the brow;
A hand rules pity as a hand rules heaven;
Hands have no tears to flow.

Should lanterns shine

Should lanterns shine, the holy face,
Caught in an octagon of unaccustomed light,
Would wither up, and any boy of love
Look twice before he fell from grace.
The features in their private dark
Are formed of flesh, but let the false day come
And from her lips the faded pigments fall,
The mummy cloths expose an ancient breast.

I have been told to reason by the heart,
But heart, like head, leads helplessly;
I have been told to reason by the pulse,
And, when it quickens, alter the actions' pace
Till field and roof lie level and the same
So fast I move defying time, the quiet gentleman
Whose beard wags in Egyptian wind.

I have heard many years of telling,
And many years should see some change.

The ball I threw while playing in the park
Has not yet reached the ground.

I have longed to move away

I have longed to move away
From the hissing of the spent lie
And the old terrors' continual cry
Growing more terrible as the day
Goes over the hill into the deep sea;
I have longed to move away
From the repetition of salutes,
For there are ghosts in the air
And ghostly echoes on paper,
And the thunder of calls and notes.

I have longed to move away but am afraid;
Some life, yet unspent, might explode
Out of the old lie burning on the ground,
And, crackling into the air, leave me half-blind.
Neither by night's ancient fear,
The parting of hat from hair,
Pursed lips at the receiver,
Shall I fall to death's feather.
By these I would not care to die,
Half convention and half lie.

Grief thief of time

Grief thief of time crawls off,
The moon-drawn grave, with the seafaring years,
The knave of pain steals off
The sea-halved faith that blew time to his knees,
The old forget the cries,
Lean time on tide and times the wind stood rough,
Call back the castaways
Riding the sea light on a sunken path,
The old forget the grief,
Hack of the cough, the hanging albatross,
Cast back the bone of youth
And salt-eyed stumble bedward where she lies
Who tossed the high tide in a time of stories
And timelessly lies loving with the thief.

Now Jack my fathers let the time-faced crook,
Death flashing from his sleeve,
With swag of bubbles in a seedy sack
Sneak down the stallion grave,
Bull's-eye the outlaw through a eunuch crack
And free the twin-boxed grief,
No silver whistles chase him down the weeks'
Dayed peaks to day to death,
These stolen bubbles have the bites of snakes
And the undead eye-teeth,
No third eye probe into a rainbow's sex
That bridged the human halves,
All shall remain and on the graveward gulf
Shape with my fathers' thieves.

And death shall have no dominion

And death shall have no dominion.
Dead men naked they shall be one
With the man in the wind and the west moon;
When their bones are picked clean and the clean bones gone,
They shall have stars at elbow and foot;
Though they go mad they shall be sane,
Though they sink through the sea they shall rise again;
Though lovers be lost love shall not;
And death shall have no dominion.

And death shall have no dominion.
Under the windings of the sea
They lying long shall not die windily;
Twisting on racks when sinews give way,
Strapped to a wheel, yet they shall not break;
Faith in their hands shall snap in two,
And the unicorn evils run them through;
Split all ends up they shan't crack;
And death shall have no dominion.

And death shall have no dominion.
No more may gulls cry at their ears
Or waves break loud on the seashores;
Where blew a flower may a flower no more
Lift its head to the blows of the rain;
Though they be mad and dead as nails,
Heads of the characters hammer through daisies;
Break in the sun till the sun breaks down,
And death shall have no dominion.

FROM
THE MAP OF LOVE
(1939)

Because the pleasure-bird whistles

Because the pleasure-bird whistles after the hot wires,
Shall the blind horse sing sweeter?
Convenient bird and beast lie lodged to suffer
The supper and knives of a mood.
In the sniffed and poured snow on the tip of the tongue of
    the year
That clouts the spittle like bubbles with broken rooms,
An enamoured man alone by the twigs of his eyes, two fires,
Camped in the drug-white shower of nerves and food,
Savours the lick of the times through a deadly wood of hair
In a wind that plucked a goose,
Nor ever, as the wild tongue breaks its tombs,
Rounds to look at the red, wagged root.
Because there stands, one story out of the bum city,
That frozen wife whose juices drift like a fixed sea
Secretly in statuary,
Shall I, struck on the hot and rocking street,
Not spin to stare at an old year
Toppling and burning in the muddle of towers and galleries
Like the mauled pictures of boys?
The salt person and blasted place
I furnish with the meat of a fable;
If the dead starve, their stomachs turn to tumble
An upright man in the antipodes
Or spray-based and rock-chested sea:
Over the past table I repeat this present grace.

We lying by seasand

We lying by seasand, watching yellow
And the grave sea, mock who deride
Who follow the red rivers, hollow
Alcove of words out of cicada shade,
For in this yellow grave of sand and sea
A calling for colour calls with the wind
That's grave and gay as grave and sea
Sleeping on either hand.
The lunar silences, the silent tide
Lapping the still canals, the dry tide-master
Ribbed between desert and water storm,
Should cure our ills of the water
With a one-coloured calm;
The heavenly music over the sand
Sounds with the grains as they hurry
Hiding the golden mountains and mansions
Of the grave, gay, seaside land.
Bound by a sovereign strip, we lie,
Watch yellow, wish for wind to blow away
The strata of the shore and drown red rock;
But wishes breed not, neither
Can we fend off rock arrival,
Lie watching yellow until the golden weather
Breaks, O my heart's blood, like a heart and hill.

After the funeral

After the funeral, mule praises, brays,
Windshake of sailshaped ears, muffle-toed tap
Tap happily of one peg in the thick
Grave's foot, blinds down the lids, the teeth in black,
The spittled eyes, the salt ponds in the sleeves,
Morning smack of the spade that wakes up sleep,
Shakes a desolate boy who slits his throat
In the dark of the coffin and sheds dry leaves,
That breaks one bone to light with a judgment clout,
After the feast of tear-stuffed time and thistles
In a room with a stuffed fox and a stale fern,
I stand, for this memorial's sake, alone
In the snivelling hours with dead, humped Ann
Whose hooded, fountain heart once fell in puddles
Round the parched worlds of Wales and drowned each sun
(Though this for her is a monstrous image blindly
Magnified out of praise; her death was a still drop;
She would not have me sinking in the holy
Flood of her heart's fame; she would lie dumb and deep
And need no druid of her broken body).
But I, Ann's bard on a raised hearth, call all
The seas to service that her wood-tongued virtue
Babble like a bellbuoy over the hymning heads,
Bow down the walls of the ferned and foxy woods
That her love sing and swing through a brown chapel,
Bless her bent spirit with four, crossing birds.

Her flesh was meek as milk, but this skyward statue
With the wild breast and blessed and giant skull
Is carved from her in a room with a wet window
In a fiercely mourning house in a crooked year.
I know her scrubbed and sour humble hands
Lie with religion in their cramp, her threadbare
Whisper in a damp word, her wits drilled hollow,
Her fist of a face died clenched on a round pain;
And sculptured Ann is seventy years of stone.
These cloud-sopped, marble hands, this monumental
Argument of the hewn voice, gesture and psalm
Storm me forever over her grave until
The stuffed lung of the fox twitch and cry Love
And the strutting fern lay seeds on the black sill.

Once it was the colour of saying

Once it was the colour of saying
Soaked my table the uglier side of a hill
With a capsized field where a school sat still
And a black and white patch of girls grew playing;
The gentle seaslides of saying I must undo
That all the charmingly drowned arise to cockcrow and kill.
When I whistled with mitching boys through a reservoir park
Where at night we stoned the cold and cuckoo
Lovers in the dirt of their leafy beds,
The shade of their trees was a word of many shades
And a lamp of lightning for the poor in the dark;
Now my saying shall be my undoing,
And every stone I wind off like a reel.

How shall my animal

How shall my animal
Whose wizard shape I trace in the cavernous skull,
Vessel of abscesses and exultation's shell,
Endure burial under the spelling wall,
The invoked, shrouding veil at the cap of the face,
Who should be furious,
Drunk as a vineyard snail, flailed like an octopus,
Roaring, crawling, quarrel
With the outside weathers,
The natural circle of the discovered skies
Draw down to its weird eyes?

How shall it magnetize,
Towards the studded male in a bent, midnight blaze
That melts the lionhead's heel and horseshoe of the heart,
A brute land in the cool top of the country days
To trot with a loud mate the haybeds of a mile,
Love and labour and kill
In quick, sweet, cruel light till the locked ground sprout
    out,
The black, burst sea rejoice,
The bowels turn turtle,
Claw of the crabbed veins squeeze from each red particle
The parched and raging voice?

Fishermen of mermen
Creep and harp on the tide, sinking their charmed, bent pin

With bridebait of gold bread, I with a living skein,
Tongue and ear in the thread, angle the temple-bound
Curl-locked and animal cavepools of spells and bone,
Trace out a tentacle,
Nailed with an open eye, in the bowl of wounds and weed
To clasp my fury on ground
And clap its great blood down;
Never shall beast be born to atlas the few seas
Or poise the day on a horn.

Sigh long, clay cold, lie shorn,
Cast high, stunned on gilled stone; sly scissors ground in frost
Clack through the thicket of strength, love hewn in pillars
    drops
With carved bird, saint, and sun, the wrackspiked maiden
    mouth
Lops, as a bush plumed with flames, the rant of the fierce eye,
Clips short the gesture of breath.
Die in red feathers when the flying heaven's cut,
And roll with the knocked earth:
Lie dry, rest robbed, my beast.
You have kicked from a dark den, leaped up the whinnying
    light,
And dug your grave in my breast.

The tombstone told

The tombstone told when she died.
Her two surnames stopped me still.
A virgin married at rest.
She married in this pouring place,
That I struck one day by luck,
Before I heard in my mother's side
Or saw in the looking-glass shell
The rain through her cold heart speak
And the sun killed in her face.
More the thick stone cannot tell.

Before she lay on a stranger's bed
With a hand plunged through her hair,
Or that rainy tongue beat back
Through the devilish years and innocent deaths
To the room of a secret child,
Among men later I heard it said
She cried her white-dressed limbs were bare
And her red lips were kissed black,
She wept in her pain and made mouths,
Talked and tore though her eyes smiled.

I who saw in a hurried film
Death and this mad heroine
Meet once on a mortal wall
Heard her speak through the chipped beak
Of the stone bird guarding her:

I died before bedtime came
But my womb was bellowing
And I felt with my bare fall
A blazing red harsh head tear up
And the dear floods of his hair.

A saint about to fall

A saint about to fall,
The stained flats of heaven hit and razed
To the kissed kite hems of his shawl,
On the last street wave praised
The unwinding, song by rock,
Of the woven wall
Of his father's house in the sands,
The vanishing of the musical ship-work and the chucked bells,
The wound-down cough of the blood-counting clock
Behind a face of hands,
On the angelic etna of the last whirring featherlands,
Wind-heeled foot in the hole of a fireball,
Hymned his shrivelling flock,
On the last rick's tip by spilled wine-wells
Sang heaven hungry and the quick
Cut Christbread spitting vinegar and all
The mazes of his praise and envious tongue were worked in
    flames and shells.

Glory cracked like a flea.
The sun-leaved holy candlewoods
Drivelled down to one singeing tree
With a stub of black buds,
The sweet, fish-gilled boats bringing blood
Lurched through a scuttled sea
With a hold of leeches and straws,
Heaven fell with his fall and one crocked bell beat the left air.

O wake in me in my house in the mud
Of the crotch of the squawking shores,
Flicked from the carbolic city puzzle in a bed of sores
The scudding base of the familiar sky,
The lofty roots of the clouds.
From an odd room in a split house stare,
Milk in your mouth, at the sour floods
That bury the sweet street slowly, see
The skull of the earth is barbed with a war of burning brains
    and hair.

Strike in the time-bomb town,
Raise the live rafters of the eardrum,
Throw your fear a parcel of stone
Through the dark asylum,
Lapped among herods wail
As their blade marches in
That the eyes are already murdered,
The stocked heart is forced, and agony has another mouth
    to feed.
O wake to see, after a noble fall,
The old mud hatch again, the horrid
Woe drip from the dishrag hands and the pressed sponge of
    the forehead,
The breath draw back like a bolt through white oil
And a stranger enter like iron.
Cry joy that this witchlike midwife second
Bullies into rough seas you so gentle
And makes with a flick of the thumb and sun
A thundering bullring of your silent and girl-circled island.

If my head hurt a hair's foot

'If my head hurt a hair's foot
Pack down the downed bone. If the unpricked ball of my breath
Bump on a spout let the bubbles jump out.
Sooner drop with the worm of the ropes round my throat
Than bully ill love in the clouted scene.

All game phrases fit your ring of a cockfight:
I'll comb the snared woods with a glove on a lamp,
Peck, sprint, dance on fountains and duck time
Before I rush in a crouch the ghost with a hammer, air,
Strike light, and bloody a loud room.

If my bunched, monkey coming is cruel
Rage me back to the making house. My hand unravel
When you sew the deep door. The bed is a cross place.
Bend, if my journey ache, direction like an arc or make
A limp and riderless shape to leap nine thinning months.'

'No. Not for Christ's dazzling bed
Or a nacreous sleep among soft particles and charms
My dear would I change my tears or your iron head.
Thrust, my daughter or son, to escape, there is none, none,
     none,
Nor when all ponderous heaven's host of waters breaks.

Now to awake husked of gestures and my joy like a cave
To the anguish and carrion, to the infant forever unfree,
O my lost love bounced from a good home;

The grain that hurries this way from the rim of the grave
Has a voice and a house, and there and here you must couch
    and cry.

Rest beyond choice in the dust-appointed grain.
At the breast stored with seas. No return
Through the waves of the fat streets nor the skeleton's thin
    ways.
The grave and my calm body are shut to your coming as
    stone,
And the endless beginning of prodigies suffers open.'

Twenty-four years

Twenty-four years remind the tears of my eyes.
(Bury the dead for fear that they walk to the grave in labour.)
In the groin of the natural doorway I crouched like a tailor
Sewing a shroud for a journey
By the light of the meat-eating sun.
Dressed to die, the sensual strut begun,
With my red veins full of money,
In the final direction of the elementary town
I advance for as long as forever is.

FROM
DEATHS AND ENTRANCES
(1946)

The conversation of prayers

The conversation of prayers about to be said
By the child going to bed and the man on the stairs
Who climbs to his dying love in her high room,
The one not caring to whom in his sleep he will move
And the other full of tears that she will be dead,

Turns in the dark on the sound they know will arise
Into the answering skies from the green ground,
From the man on the stairs and the child by his bed.
The sound about to be said in the two prayers
For the sleep in a safe land and the love who dies

Will be the same grief flying. Whom shall they calm?
Shall the child sleep unharmed or the man be crying?
The conversation of prayers about to be said
Turns on the quick and the dead, and the man on the stairs
Tonight shall find no dying but alive and warm

In the fire of his care his love in the high room.
And the child not caring to whom he climbs his prayer
Shall drown in a grief as deep as his true grave,
And mark the dark eyed wave, through the eyes of sleep,
Dragging him up the stairs to one who lies dead.

Poem in October

It was my thirtieth year to heaven
Woke to my hearing from harbour and neighbour wood
   And the mussel pooled and the heron
        Priested shore
     The morning beckon
With water praying and call of seagull and rook
And the knock of sailing boats on the net webbed wall
     Myself to set foot
       That second
   In the still sleeping town and set forth.

   My birthday began with the water-
Birds and the birds of the winged trees flying my name
   Above the farms and the white horses
        And I rose
     In rainy autumn
And walked abroad in a shower of all my days.
High tide and the heron dived when I took the road
     Over the border
       And the gates
   Of the town closed as the town awoke.

   A springful of larks in a rolling
Cloud and the roadside bushes brimming with whistling
  Blackbirds and the sun of October
       Summery
     On the hill's shoulder,

Here were fond climates and sweet singers suddenly
Come in the morning where I wandered and listened
    To the rain wringing
        Wind blow cold
  In the wood faraway under me.

  Pale rain over the dwindling harbour
And over the sea wet church the size of a snail
    With its horns through mist and the castle
        Brown as owls
    But all the gardens
Of spring and summer were blooming in the tall tales
Beyond the border and under the lark full cloud.
    There could I marvel
        My birthday
  Away but the weather turned around.

  It turned away from the blithe country
And down the other air and the blue altered sky
    Streamed again a wonder of summer
        With apples
    Pears and red currants
And I saw in the turning so clearly a child's
Forgotten mornings when he walked with his mother
    Through the parables
        Of sun light
  And the legends of the green chapels

  And the twice told fields of infancy
That his tears burned my cheeks and his heart moved in mine.
    These were the woods the river and sea

    Where a boy
    In the listening
Summertime of the dead whispered the truth of his joy
To the trees and the stones and the fish in the tide.
    And the mystery
        Sang alive
    Still in the water and singingbirds.

    And there could I marvel my birthday
Away but the weather turned around. And the true
    Joy of the long dead child sang burning
            In the sun.
    It was my thirtieth
Year to heaven stood there then in the summer noon
Though the town below lay leaved with October blood.
    O may my heart's truth
        Still be sung
    On this high hill in a year's turning.

This side of the truth

(FOR LLEWELYN)

This side of the truth,
You may not see, my son,
King of your blue eyes
In the blinding country of youth,
That all is undone,
Under the unminding skies,
Of innocence and guilt
Before you move to make
One gesture of the heart or head,
Is gathered and spilt
Into the winding dark
Like the dust of the dead.

Good and bad, two ways
Of moving about your death
By the grinding sea,
King of your heart in the blind days,
Blow away like breath,
Go crying through you and me
And the souls of all men
Into the innocent
Dark, and the guilty dark, and good
Death, and bad death, and then
In the last element
Fly like the stars' blood,

Like the sun's tears,
Like the moon's seed, rubbish
And fire, the flying rant
Of the sky, king of your six years.
And the wicked wish,
Down the beginning of plants
And animals and birds,
Water and light, the earth and sky,
Is cast before you move,
And all your deeds and words,
Each truth, each lie,
Die in unjudging love.

Love in the Asylum

A stranger has come
To share my room in the house not right in the head,
A girl mad as birds

Bolting the night of the door with her arm her plume.
Strait in the mazed bed
She deludes the heaven-proof house with entering clouds

Yet she deludes with walking the nightmarish room,
At large as the dead,
Or rides the imagined oceans of the male wards.

She has come possessed
Who admits the delusive light through the bouncing wall,
Possessed by the skies

She sleeps in the narrow trough yet she walks the dust
Yet raves at her will
On the madhouse boards worn thin by my walking tears.

And taken by light in her arms at long and dear last
I may without fail
Suffer the first vision that set fire to the stars.

The hunchback in the park

The hunchback in the park
A solitary mister
Propped between trees and water
From the opening of the garden lock
That lets the trees and water enter
Until the Sunday sombre bell at dark

Eating bread from a newspaper
Drinking water from the chained cup
That the children filled with gravel
In the fountain basin where I sailed my ship
Slept at night in a dog kennel
But nobody chained him up.

Like the park birds he came early
Like the water he sat down
And Mister they called Hey mister
The truant boys from the town
Running when he had heard them clearly
On out of sound

Past lake and rockery
Laughing when he shook his paper
Hunchbacked in mockery
Through the loud zoo of the willow groves
Dodging the park keeper
With his stick that picked up leaves.

And the old dog sleeper
Alone between nurses and swans
While the boys among willows
Made the tigers jump out of their eyes
To roar on the rockery stones
And the groves were blue with sailors

Made all day until bell time
A woman figure without fault
Straight as a young elm
Straight and tall from his crooked bones
That she might stand in the night
After the locks and chains

All night in the unmade park
After the railings and shrubberies
The birds the grass the trees the lake
And the wild boys innocent as strawberries
Had followed the hunchback
To his kennel in the dark.

Deaths and Entrances

On almost the incendiary eve
    Of several near deaths,
When one at the great least of your best loved
    And always known must leave
Lions and fires of his flying breath,
    Of your immortal friends
Who'd raise the organs of the counted dust
    To shoot and sing your praise,
One who called deepest down shall hold his peace
    That cannot sink or cease
    Endlessly to his wound
In many married London's estranging grief.

On almost the incendiary eve
    When at your lips and keys,
Locking, unlocking, the murdered strangers weave,
    One who is most unknown,
Your polestar neighbour, sun of another street,
    Will dive up to his tears.
He'll bathe his raining blood in the male sea
    Who strode for your own dead
And wind his globe out of your water thread
    And load the throats of shells
    With every cry since light
Flashed first across his thunderclapping eyes.

On almost the incendiary eve
    Of deaths and entrances,
When near and strange wounded on London's waves
    Have sought your single grave,
One enemy, of many, who knows well
    Your heart is luminous
In the watched dark, quivering through locks and caves,
    Will pull the thunderbolts
To shut the sun, plunge, mount your darkened keys
    And sear just riders back,
    Until that one loved least
Looms the last Samson of your zodiac.

On a Wedding Anniversary

The sky is torn across
This ragged anniversary of two
Who moved for three years in tune
Down the long walks of their vows.

Now their love lies a loss
And Love and his patients roar on a chain;
From every true or crater
Carrying cloud, Death strikes their house.

Too late in the wrong rain
They come together whom their love parted:
The windows pour into their heart
And the doors burn in their brain.

On the Marriage of a Virgin

Waking alone in a multitude of loves when morning's light
Surprised in the opening of her nightlong eyes
His golden yesterday asleep upon the iris
And this day's sun leapt up the sky out of her thighs
Was miraculous virginity old as loaves and fishes,
Though the moment of a miracle is unending lightning
And the shipyards of Galilee's footprints hide a navy of doves.

No longer will the vibrations of the sun desire on
Her deepsea pillow where once she married alone,
Her heart all ears and eyes, lips catching the avalanche
Of the golden ghost who ringed with his streams her mercury
    bone,
Who under the lids of her windows hoisted his golden luggage,
For a man sleeps where fire leapt down and she learns
    through his arm
That other sun, the jealous coursing of the unrivalled blood.

In my craft or sullen art

In my craft or sullen art
Exercised in the still night
When only the moon rages
And the lovers lie abed
With all their griefs in their arms,
I labour by singing light
Not for ambition or bread
Or the strut and trade of charms
On the ivory stages
But for the common wages
Of their most secret heart.

Not for the proud man apart
From the raging moon I write
On these spindrift pages
Nor for the towering dead
With their nightingales and psalms
But for the lovers, their arms
Round the griefs of the ages,
Who pay no praise or wages
Nor heed my craft or art.

Ceremony After a Fire Raid

I

Myselves
The grievers
Grieve
Among the street burned to tireless death
A child of a few hours
With its kneading mouth
Charred on the black breast of the grave
The mother dug, and its arms full of fires.

Begin
With singing
Sing
Darkness kindled back into beginning
When the caught tongue nodded blind,
A star was broken
Into the centuries of the child
Myselves grieve now, and miracles cannot atone.

Forgive
Us forgive
Give
Us your death that myselves the believers
May hold it in a great flood
Till the blood shall spurt,
And the dust shall sing like a bird
As the grains blow, as your death grows, through our heart.

Crying
Your dying
Cry,
Child beyond cockcrow, by the fire-dwarfed
Street we chant the flying sea
In the body bereft.
Love is the last light spoken. Oh
Seed of sons in the loin of the black husk left.

I I

I know not whether
Adam or Eve, the adorned holy bullock
Or the white ewe lamb
Or the chosen virgin
Laid in her snow
On the altar of London,
Was the first to die
In the cinder of the little skull,
O bride and bride groom
O Adam and Eve together
Lying in the lull
Under the sad breast of the head stone
White as the skeleton
Of the garden of Eden.

I know the legend
Of Adam and Eve is never for a second
Silent in my service
Over the dead infants
Over the one

Child who was priest and servants,
Word, singers, and tongue
In the cinder of the little skull,
Who was the serpent's
Night fall and the fruit like a sun,
Man and woman undone,
Beginning crumbled back to darkness
Bare as the nurseries
Of the garden of wilderness.

III

Into the organpipes and steeples
Of the luminous cathedrals,
Into the weathercocks' molten mouths
Rippling in twelve-winded circles,
Into the dead clock burning the hour
Over the urn of sabbaths
Over the whirling ditch of daybreak
Over the sun's hovel and the slum of fire
And the golden pavements laid in requiems,
Into the cauldrons of the statuary,
Into the bread in a wheatfield of flames,
Into the wine burning like brandy,
The masses of the sea
The masses of the sea under
The masses of the infant-bearing sea
Erupt, fountain, and enter to utter for ever
Glory glory glory
The sundering ultimate kingdom of genesis' thunder.

Once below a time

I

Once below a time,
When my pinned-around-the-spirit
Cut-to-measure flesh bit,
Suit for a serial sum
On the first of each hardship,
My paid-for slaved-for own too late
In love torn breeches and blistered jacket
On the snapping rims of the ashpit,
In grottoes I worked with birds,
Spiked with a mastiff collar,
Tasselled in cellar and snipping shop
Or decked on a cloud swallower,

Then swift from a bursting sea with bottlecork boats
And out-of-perspective sailors,
In common clay clothes disguised as scales,
As a he-god's paddling water skirts,
I astounded the sitting tailors,
I set back the clock faced tailors,

Then, bushily swanked in bear wig and tails,
Hopping hot leaved and feathered
From the kangaroo foot of the earth,

From the chill, silent centre
Trailing the frost bitten cloth,
Up through the lubber crust of Wales
I rocketed to astonish
The flashing needle rock of squatters,
The criers of Shabby and Shorten,
The famous stitch droppers.

II

My silly suit, hardly yet suffered for,
Around some coffin carrying
Birdman or told ghost I hung.
And the owl hood, the heel hider,
Claw fold and hole for the rotten
Head, deceived, I believed, my maker,

The cloud perched tailors' master with nerves for cotton.
On the old seas from stories, thrashing my wings,
Combing with antlers, Columbus on fire,
I was pierced by the idol tailor's eyes,
Glared through shark mask and navigating head,
Cold Nansen's beak on a boat full of gongs,

To the boy of common thread,
The bright pretender, the ridiculous sea dandy
With dry flesh and earth for adorning and bed.
It was sweet to drown in the readymade handy water
With my cherry capped dangler green as seaweed
Summoning a child's voice from a webfoot stone,

Never never oh never to regret the bugle I wore
On my cleaving arm as I blasted in a wave.

Now shown and mostly bare I would lie down,
Lie down, lie down and live
As quiet as a bone.

When I woke

When I woke, the town spoke.
Birds and clocks and cross bells
Dinned aside the coiling crowd,
The reptile profligates in a flame,
Spoilers and pokers of sleep,
The next-door sea dispelled
Frogs and satans and woman-luck,
While a man outside with a billhook,
Up to his head in his blood,
Cutting the morning off,
The warm-veined double of Time
And his scarving beard from a book,
Slashed down the last snake as though
It were a wand or subtle bough,
Its tongue peeled in the wrap of a leaf.

Every morning I make,
God in bed, good and bad,
After a water-face walk,
The death-stagged scatter-breath
Mammoth and sparrowfall
Everybody's earth.
Where birds ride like leaves and boats like ducks
I heard, this morning, waking,
Crossly out of the town noises
A voice in the erected air,
No prophet-progeny of mine,

Cry my sea town was breaking.
No Time, spoke the clocks, no God, rang the bells,
I drew the white sheet over the islands
And the coins on my eyelids sang like shells.

Among those Killed in the Dawn Raid was a Man Aged a Hundred

When the morning was waking over the war
He put on his clothes and stepped out and he died,
The locks yawned loose and a blast blew them wide,
He dropped where he loved on the burst pavement stone
And the funeral grains of the slaughtered floor.
Tell his street on its back he stopped a sun
And the craters of his eyes grew springshoots and fire
When all the keys shot from the locks, and rang.
Dig no more for the chains of his grey-haired heart.
The heavenly ambulance drawn by a wound
Assembling waits for the spade's ring on the cage.
O keep his bones away from that common cart,
The morning is flying on the wings of his age
And a hundred storks perch on the sun's right hand.

Lie still, sleep becalmed

Lie still, sleep becalmed, sufferer with the wound
In the throat, burning and turning. All night afloat
On the silent sea we have heard the sound
That came from the wound wrapped in the salt sheet.

Under the mile off moon we trembled listening
To the sea sound flowing like blood from the loud wound
And when the salt sheet broke in a storm of singing
The voices of all the drowned swam on the wind.

Open a pathway through the slow sad sail,
Throw wide to the wind the gates of the wandering boat
For my voyage to begin to the end of my wound,
We heard the sea sound sing, we saw the salt sheet tell.
Lie still, sleep becalmed, hide the mouth in the throat,
Or we shall obey, and ride with you through the drowned.

Vision and Prayer

I

Who
Are you
Who is born
In the next room
So loud to my own
That I can hear the womb
Opening and the dark run
Over the ghost and the dropped son
Behind the wall thin as a wren's bone?
In the birth bloody room unknown
To the burn and turn of time
And the heart print of man
Bows no baptism
But dark alone
Blessing on
The wild
Child.

I
Must lie
Still as stone
By the wren bone
Wall hearing the moan
Of the mother hidden
And the shadowed head of pain
Casting tomorrow like a thorn
And the midwives of miracle sing
Until the turbulent new born
Burns me his name and his flame
And the winged wall is torn
By his torrid crown
And the dark thrown
From his loin
To bright
Light.

When

The wren

Bone writhes down

And the first dawn

Furied by his stream

Swarms on the kingdom come

Of the dazzler of heaven

And the splashed mothering maiden

Who bore him with a bonfire in

His mouth and rocked him like a storm

I shall run lost in sudden

Terror and shining from

The once hooded room

Crying in vain

In the caldron

Of his

Kiss

In
The spin
Of the sun
In the spuming
Cyclone of his wing
For I was lost who am
Crying at the man drenched throne
In the first fury of his stream
And the lightnings of adoration
Back to black silence melt and mourn
For I was lost who have come
To dumbfounding haven
And the finding one
And the high noon
Of his wound
Blinds my
Cry.

There
Crouched bare
In the shrine
Of his blazing
Breast I shall waken
To the judge blown bedlam
Of the uncaged sea bottom
The cloud climb of the exhaling tomb
And the bidden dust upsailing
With his flame in every grain.
O spiral of ascension
From the vultured urn
Of the morning
Of man when
The land
A n d

The

Born sea

Praised the sun

The finding one

And upright Adam

Sang upon origin!

O the wings of the children!

The woundward flight of the ancient

Young from the canyons of oblivion!

The sky stride of the always slain

In battle! the happening

Of saints to their vision!

The world winding home!

And the whole pain

Flows open

And I

Die.

In the name of the lost who glory in
The swinish plains of carrion
Under the burial song
Of the birds of burden
Heavy with the drowned
And the green dust
And bearing
The ghost
From
The ground
Like pollen
On the black plume
And the beak of slime
I pray though I belong
Not wholly to that lamenting
Brethren for joy has moved within
The inmost marrow of my heart bone

That he who learns now the sun and moon
Of his mother's milk may return
Before the lips blaze and bloom
To the birth bloody room
Behind the wall's wren
Bone and be dumb
And the womb
That bore
For
All men
The adored
Infant light or
The dazzling prison
Yawn to his upcoming.
In the name of the wanton
Lost on the unchristened mountain
In the centre of dark I pray him

That he let the dead lie though they moan
For his briared hands to hoist them
To the shrine of his world's wound
And the blood drop's garden
Endure the stone
Blind host to sleep
In the dark
And deep
Rock
Awake
No heartbone
But let it break
On the mountain crown
Unbidden by the sun
And the beating dust be blown
Down to the river rooting plain
Under the night forever falling.

Forever falling night is a known
Star and country to the legion
Of sleepers whose tongue I toll
To mourn his deluging
Light through sea and soil
And we have come
To know all
P l a c e s
Ways
M a z e s
P a s s a g e s
Quarters and graves
Of the endless fall.
Now common lazarus
Of the charting sleepers prays
Never to awake and arise
For the country of death is the heart's size

And the star of the lost the shape of the eyes.
In the name of the fatherless
In the name of the unborn
And the undesirers
Of midwiving morning's
Hands or instruments
O in the name
Of no one
Now or
No
One to
Be I pray
May the crimson
Sun spin a grave grey
And the colour of clay
Stream upon his martyrdom
In the interpreted evening
And the known dark of the earth amen.

I turn the corner of prayer and burn
In a blessing of the sudden
Sun. In the name of the damned
I would turn back and run
To the hidden land
But the loud sun
Christens down
The sky.
I
Am found.
O let him
Scald me and drown
Me in his world's wound.
His lightning answers my
Cry. My voice burns in his hand.
Now I am lost in the blinding
One. The sun roars at the prayer's end.

Fern Hill

Now as I was young and easy under the apple boughs
About the lilting house and happy as the grass was green,
    The night above the dingle starry,
        Time let me hail and climb
    Golden in the heydays of his eyes,
And honoured among wagons I was prince of the apple towns
And once below a time I lordly had the trees and leaves
        Trail with daisies and barley
    Down the rivers of the windfall light.

And as I was green and carefree, famous among the barns
About the happy yard and singing as the farm was home,
    In the sun that is young once only,
        Time let me play and be
    Golden in the mercy of his means,
And green and golden I was huntsman and herdsman, the calves
Sang to my horn, the foxes on the hills barked clear and cold,
        And the sabbath rang slowly
    In the pebbles of the holy streams.

All the sun long it was running, it was lovely, the hay
Fields high as the house, the tunes from the chimneys, it was air
    And playing, lovely and watery
        And fire green as grass.
    And nightly under the simple stars
As I rode to sleep the owls were bearing the farm away,
All the moon long I heard, blessed among stables, the nightjars
        Flying with the ricks, and the horses
            Flashing into the dark.

And then to awake, and the farm, like a wanderer white
With the dew, come back, the cock on his shoulder: it was all
    Shining, it was Adam and maiden,
      The sky gathered again
    And the sun grew round that very day.
So it must have been after the birth of the simple light
In the first, spinning place, the spellbound horses walking warm
    Out of the whinnying green stable
      On to the fields of praise.

And honoured among foxes and pheasants by the gay house
Under the new made clouds and happy as the heart was long,
    In the sun born over and over,
      I ran my heedless ways,
    My wishes raced through the house high hay
And nothing I cared, at my sky blue trades, that time allows
In all his tuneful turning so few and such morning songs
    Before the children green and golden
      Follow him out of grace,

Nothing I cared, in the lamb white days, that time would take me
Up to the swallow thronged loft by the shadow of my hand,
    In the moon that is always rising,
      Nor that riding to sleep
    I should hear him fly with the high fields
And wake to the farm forever fled from the childless land.
Oh as I was young and easy in the mercy of his means,
      Time held me green and dying
    Though I sang in my chains like the sea.

FROM
IN COUNTRY SLEEP
(1952)

In Country Sleep

I

Never and never, my girl riding far and near
In the land of the hearthstone tales, and spelled asleep,
Fear or believe that the wolf in a sheepwhite hood
Loping and bleating roughly and blithely shall leap,
     My dear, my dear,
Out of a lair in the flocked leaves in the dew dipped year
To eat your heart in the house in the rosy wood.

Sleep, good, for ever, slow and deep, spelled rare and wise,
My girl ranging the night in the rose and shire
Of the hobnail tales: no gooseherd or swine will turn
Into a homestall king or hamlet of fire
     And prince of ice
To court the honeyed heart from your side before sunrise
In a spinney of ringed boys and ganders, spike and burn,

Nor the innocent lie in the rooting dingle wooed
And staved, and riven among plumes my rider weep.
From the broomed witch's spume you are shielded by fern
And flower of country sleep and the greenwood keep.
     Lie fast and soothed,
Safe be and smooth from the bellows of the rushy brood.
Never, my girl, until tolled to sleep by the stern

Bell believe or fear that the rustic shade or spell
Shall harrow and snow the blood while you ride wide and near,
For who unmanningly haunts the mountain ravened eaves
Or skulks in the dell moon but moonshine echoing clear
From the starred well?
A hill touches an angel. Out of a saint's cell
The nightbird lauds through nunneries and domes of leaves

Her robin breasted tree, three Marys in the rays.
Sanctum sanctorum the animal eye of the wood
In the rain telling its beads, and the gravest ghost
The owl at its knelling. Fox and holt kneel before blood.
Now the tales praise
The star rise at pasture and nightlong the fables graze
On the lord's table of the bowing grass. Fear most

For ever of all not the wolf in his baaing hood
Nor the tusked prince, in the ruttish farm, at the rind
And mire of love, but the Thief as meek as the dew.
The country is holy: O bide in that country kind,
Know the green good,
Under the prayer wheeling moon in the rosy wood
Be shielded by chant and flower and gay may you

Lie in grace. Sleep spelled at rest in the lowly house
In the squirrel nimble grove, under linen and thatch
And star: held and blessed, though you scour the high four
Winds, from the dousing shade and the roarer at the latch,
Cool in your vows.
Yet out of the beaked, web dark and the pouncing boughs
Be you sure the Thief will seek a way sly and sure

And sly as snow and meek as dew blown to the thorn,
This night and each vast night until the stern bell talks
In the tower and tolls to sleep over the stalls
Of the hearthstone tales my own, lost love; and the soul walks
              The waters shorn.
This night and each night since the falling star you were born,
Ever and ever he finds a way, as the snow falls,

As the rain falls, hail on the fleece, as the vale mist rides
Through the haygold stalls, as the dew falls on the wind-
Milled dust of the apple tree and the pounded islands
Of the morning leaves, as the star falls, as the winged
              Apple seed glides,
And falls, and flowers in the yawning wound at our sides,
As the world falls, silent as the cyclone of silence.

I I

Night and the reindeer on the clouds above the haycocks
And the wings of the great roc ribboned for the fair!
The leaping saga of prayer! And high, there, on the hare-
              Heeled winds the rooks
Cawing from their black bethels soaring, the holy books
Of birds! Among the cocks like fire the red fox

Burning! Night and the vein of birds in the winged, sloe wrist
Of the wood! Pastoral beat of blood through the laced leaves!
The stream from the priest black wristed spinney and sleeves
              Of thistling frost

Of the nightingale's din and tale! The upgiven ghost
Of the dingle torn to singing and the surpliced

Hill of cypresses! The din and tale in the skimmed
Yard of the buttermilk rain on the pail! The sermon
Of blood! The bird loud vein! The saga from mermen
                    To seraphim
Leaping! The gospel rooks! All tell, this night, of him
Who comes as red as the fox and sly as the heeled wind.

Illumination of music! the lulled black backed
Gull, on the wave with sand in its eyes! And the foal moves
Through the shaken greensward lake, silent, on moonshod
    hooves,
                    In the winds' wakes.
Music of elements, that a miracle makes!
Earth, air, water, fire, singing into the white act,

The haygold haired, my love asleep, and the rift blue
Eyed, in the haloed house, in her rareness and hilly
High riding, held and blessed and true, and so stilly
                    Lying the sky
Might cross its planets, the bell weep, night gather her eyes,
The Thief fall on the dead like the willynilly dew,

Only for the turning of the earth in her holy
Heart! Slyly, slowly, hearing the wound in her side go
Round the sun, he comes to my love like the designed snow,
                    And truly he
Flows to the strand of flowers like the dew's ruly sea,
And surely he sails like the ship shape clouds. Oh he

Comes designed to my love to steal not her tide raking
Wound, nor her riding high, nor her eyes, nor kindled hair,
But her faith that each vast night and the saga of prayer
                    He comes to take
Her faith that this last night for his unsacred sake
He comes to leave her in the lawless sun awaking

Naked and forsaken to grieve he will not come.
Ever and ever by all your vows believe and fear
My dear this night he comes and night without end my dear
                    Since you were born:
And you shall wake, from country sleep, this dawn and each
    first dawn,
Your faith as deathless as the outcry of the ruled sun.

Over Sir John's hill

Over Sir John's hill,
The hawk on fire hangs still;
In a hoisted cloud, at drop of dusk, he pulls to his claws
And gallows, up the rays of his eyes the small birds of the bay
And the shrill child's play
Wars
Of the sparrows and such who swansing, dusk, in wrangling
    hedges.
And blithely they squawk
To fiery tyburn over the wrestle of elms until
The flash the noosed hawk
Crashes, and slowly the fishing holy stalking heron
In the river Towy below bows his tilted headstone.

Flash, and the plumes crack,
And a black cap of jack-
Daws Sir John's just hill dons, and again the gulled birds hare
To the hawk on fire, the halter height, over Towy's fins,
In a whack of wind.
There
Where the elegiac fisherbird stabs and paddles
In the pebbly dab filled
Shallow and sedge, and 'dilly dilly,' calls the loft hawk,
'Come and be killed,'
I open the leaves of the water at a passage
Of psalms and shadows among the pincered sandcrabs
    prancing

And read, in a shell,
Death clear as a buoy's bell:
All praise of the hawk on fire in hawk-eyed dusk be sung,
When his viperish fuse hangs looped with flames under the
    brand
Wing, and blest shall
Young
Green chickens of the bay and bushes cluck, 'dilly dilly,
Come let us die.'
We grieve as the blithe birds, never again, leave shingle and elm,
The heron and I,
I young Aesop fabling to the near night by the dingle
Of eels, saint heron hymning in the shell-hung distant

Crystal harbour vale
Where the sea cobbles sail,
And wharves of water where the walls dance and the white
    cranes stilt.
It is the heron and I, under judging Sir John's elmed
Hill, tell-tale the knelled
Guilt
Of the led-astray birds whom God, for their breast of whistles,
Have mercy on,
God in his whirlwind silence save, who marks the sparrows hail,
For their souls' song.
Now the heron grieves in the weeded verge. Through windows
Of dusk and water I see the tilting whispering

Heron, mirrored, go,
As the snapt feathers snow,

Fishing in the tear of the Towy. Only a hoot owl
Hollows, a grassblade blown in cupped hands, in the looted
    elms,
And no green cocks or hens
Shout
Now on Sir John's hill. The heron, ankling the scaly
Lowlands of the waves,
Makes all the music; and I who hear the tune of the slow,
Wear-willow river, grave,
Before the lunge of the night, the notes on this time-shaken
Stone for the sake of the souls of the slain birds sailing.

Poem on his Birthday

In the mustardseed sun,
By full tilt river and switchback sea
    Where the cormorants scud,
In his house on stilts high among beaks
    And palavers of birds
This sandgrain day in the bent bay's grave
    He celebrates and spurns
His driftwood thirty-fifth wind turned age;
    Herons spire and spear.

Under and round him go
Flounders, gulls, on their cold, dying trails,
    Doing what they are told,
Curlews aloud in the congered waves
    Work at their ways to death,
And the rhymer in the long tongued room,
    Who tolls his birthday bell,
Toils towards the ambush of his wounds;
    Herons, steeple stemmed, bless.

In the thistledown fall,
He sings towards anguish; finches fly
    in the claw tracks of hawks
On a seizing sky; small fishes glide
    Through wynds and shells of drowned
Ship towns to pasture of otters. He
    In his slant, racking house
And the hewn coils of his trade perceives
    Herons walk in their shroud,

The livelong river's robe
Of minnows wreathing around their prayer;
   And far at sea he knows,
Who slaves to his crouched, eternal end
   Under a serpent cloud,
Dolphins dive in their turnturtle dust,
   The rippled seals streak down
To kill and their own tide daubing blood
   Slides good in the sleek mouth.

   In a cavernous, swung
Wave's silence, wept white angelus knells.
   Thirty-five bells sing struck
On skull and scar where his loves lie wrecked,
   Steered by the falling stars.
And tomorrow weeps in a blind cage
   Terror will rage apart
Before chains break to a hammer flame
   And love unbolts the dark

   And freely he goes lost
In the unknown, famous light of great
   And fabulous, dear God.
Dark is a way and light is a place,
   Heaven that never was
Nor will be ever is always true,
   And, in that brambled void,
Plenty as blackberries in the woods
   The dead grow for His joy.

There he might wander bare
With the spirits of the horseshoe bay
  Or the stars' seashore dead,
Marrow of eagles, the roots of whales
  And wishbones of wild geese,
With blessed, unborn God and His Ghost,
  And every soul His priest,
Gulled and chanter in young Heaven's fold
  Be at cloud quaking peace,

  But dark is a long way.
He, on the earth of the night, alone
  With all the living, prays,
Who knows the rocketing wind will blow
  The bones out of the hills,
And the scythed boulders bleed, and the last
  Rage shattered waters kick
Masts and fishes to the still quick stars,
  Faithlessly unto Him

  Who is the light of old
And air shaped Heaven where souls grow wild
  As horses in the foam:
Oh, let me midlife mourn by the shrined
  And druid herons' vows
The voyage to ruin I must run,
  Dawn ships clouted aground,
Yet, though I cry with tumbledown tongue,
  Count my blessings aloud:

Four elements and five
Senses, and man a spirit in love
    Tangling through this spun slime
To his nimbus bell cool kingdom come
    And the lost, moonshine domes,
And the sea that hides his secret selves
    Deep in its black, base bones,
Lulling of spheres in the seashell flesh,
    And this last blessing most,

    That the closer I move
To death, one man through his sundered hulks,
    The louder the sun blooms
And the tusked, ramshackling sea exults;
    And every wave of the way
And gale I tackle, the whole world then
    With more triumphant faith
Than ever was since the world was said
    Spins its morning of praise,

    I hear the bouncing hills
Grow larked and greener at berry brown
    Fall and the dew larks sing
Taller this thunderclap spring, and how
    More spanned with angels ride
The mansouled fiery islands! Oh,
    Holier then their eyes,
And my shining men no more alone
    As I sail out to die.

Do not go gentle into that good night

Do not go gentle into that good night,
Old age should burn and rave at close of day;
Rage, rage against the dying of the light.

Though wise men at their end know dark is right,
Because their words had forked no lightning they
Do not go gentle into that good night.

Good men, the last wave by, crying how bright
Their frail deeds might have danced in a green bay,
Rage, rage against the dying of the light.

Wild men who caught and sang the sun in flight,
And learn, too late, they grieved it on its way,
Do not go gentle into that good night.

Grave men, near death, who see with blinding sight
Blind eyes could blaze like meteors and be gay,
Rage, rage against the dying of the light.

And you, my father, there on the sad height,
Curse, bless, me now with your fierce tears, I pray.
Do not go gentle into that good night.
Rage, rage against the dying of the light.

LAST POEMS

In Country Heaven

Always when He, in country heaven,
　　(Whom my heart hears),
Crosses the breast of the praising east and kneels,
　　Humble in all his planets,
　　And weeps on the abasing crest,

Then in the last ward and joy of beasts and birds
　　And the canonized valley
　　Where all sings, that was made and is dead,
　　And the angels whirr like pheasants
　　　Through naves of leaves,

Light and His tears dewfall together
　　(O hand in hand)
Out of the pierced eyes and the cataract sky,
　　He cries his blood, and the suns
　　Dissolve and run down the raggèd

Gutters of his face: Heaven is blind and black.

Elegy

Too proud to die, broken and blind he died
The darkest way, and did not turn away,
A cold, kind man brave in his burning pride

On that darkest day. Oh, forever may
He live lightly, at last, on the last, crossed
Hill, and there grow young, under the grass, in love,

Among the long flocks, and never lie lost
Or still all the days of his death, though above
All he longed all dark for his mother's breast

Which was rest and dust, and in the kind ground
The darkest justice of death, blind and unblessed.
Let him find no rest but be fathered and found,

I prayed in the crouching room, by his blind bed,
In the muted house, one minute before
Noon, and night, and light. The rivers of the dead

Moved in his poor hand I held, and I saw
Through his faded eyes to the roots of the sea.
Go calm to your crucifixed hill, I told

The air that drew away from him.

Prologue

This day winding down now
At God speeded summer's end
In the torrent salmon sun,
In my seashaken house
On a breakneck of rocks
Tangled with chirrup and fruit,
Froth, flute, fin and quill
At a wood's dancing hoof,
By scummed, starfish sands
With their fishwife cross
Gulls, pipers, cockles, and sails,
Out there, crow black, men
Tackled with clouds, who kneel
To the sunset nets,
Geese nearly in heaven, boys
Stabbing, and herons, and shells
That speak seven seas,
Eternal waters away
From the cities of nine
Days' night whose towers will catch
In the religious wind
Like stalks of tall, dry straw,
At poor peace I sing
To you, strangers, (though song
Is a burning and crested act,
The fire of birds in
The world's turning wood,

For my sawn, splay sounds),
Out of these seathumbed leaves
That will fly and fall
Like leaves of trees and as soon
Crumble and undie
Into the dogdayed night.
Seaward the salmon, sucked sun slips,
And the dumb swans drub blue
My dabbed bay's dusk, as I hack
This rumpus of shapes
For you to know
How I, a spinning man,
Glory also this star, bird
Roared, sea born, man torn, blood blest.
Hark: I trumpet the place,
From fish to jumping hill! Look:
I build my bellowing ark
To the best of my love
As the flood begins,
Out of the fountainhead
Of fear, rage red, manalive,
Molten and mountainous to stream
Over the wound asleep
Sheep white hollow farms

To Wales in my arms.
Hoo, there, in castle keep,
You king singsong owls, who moonbeam

The flickering runs and dive
The dingle furred deer dead!
Huloo, on plumbed bryns,
O my ruffled ring dove
In the hooting, nearly dark
With Welsh and reverent rook,
Coo rooing the woods' praise,
Who moons her blue notes from her nest
Down to the curlew herd!
Ho, hullaballoing clan
Agape, with woe
In your beaks, on the gabbing capes!
Heigh, on horseback hill, jack
Whisking hare! who
Hears, there, this fox light, my flood ship's
Clangour as I hew and smite
(A clash of anvils for my
Hubbub and fiddle, this tune
On a tongued puffball)
But animals thick as thieves
On God's rough tumbling grounds
(Hail to His beasthood!).
Beasts who sleep good and thin,
Hist, in hogsback woods! The haystacked
Hollow farms in a throng
Of waters cluck and cling,
And barnroofs cockcrow war!
O kingdom of neighbours, finned
Felled and quilled, flash to my patch
Work ark and the moonshine

Drinking Noah of the bay,
With pelt, and scale, and fleece:
Only the drowned deep bells
Of sheep and churches noise
Poor peace as the sun sets
And dark shoals every holy field.
We will ride out alone, and then,
Under the stars of Wales,
Cry, Multitudes of arks! Across
The water lidded lands,
Manned with their loves they'll move,
Like wooden islands, hill to hill.
Huloo, my prowed dove with a flute!
Ahoy, old, sea-legged fox,
Tom tit and Dai mouse!
My ark sings in the sun
At God speeded summer's end
And the flood flowers now.

A FINAL PRAYER

Reverend Eli Jenkins' Prayer

(FROM *UNDER MILK WOOD*, 1953)

Every morning when I wake,
Dear Lord, a little prayer I make,
O please to keep Thy lovely eye
On all poor creatures born to die

And every evening at sun-down
I ask a blessing on the town,
For whether we last the night or no
I'm sure is always touch-and-go.

We are not wholly bad or good
Who live our lives under Milk Wood,
And Thou, I know, wilt be the first
To see our best side, not our worst.

O let us see another day!
Bless us all this night, I pray,
And to the sun we all will bow
And say, good-bye—but just for now!

DYLAN MARLAIS THOMAS
BORN AT 5 CWMDONKIN DRIVE, SWANSEA
27TH OCTOBER 1914

DIED AT ST VINCENT'S HOSPITAL, NEW YORK
AGED THIRTY-NINE
9TH NOVEMBER 1953

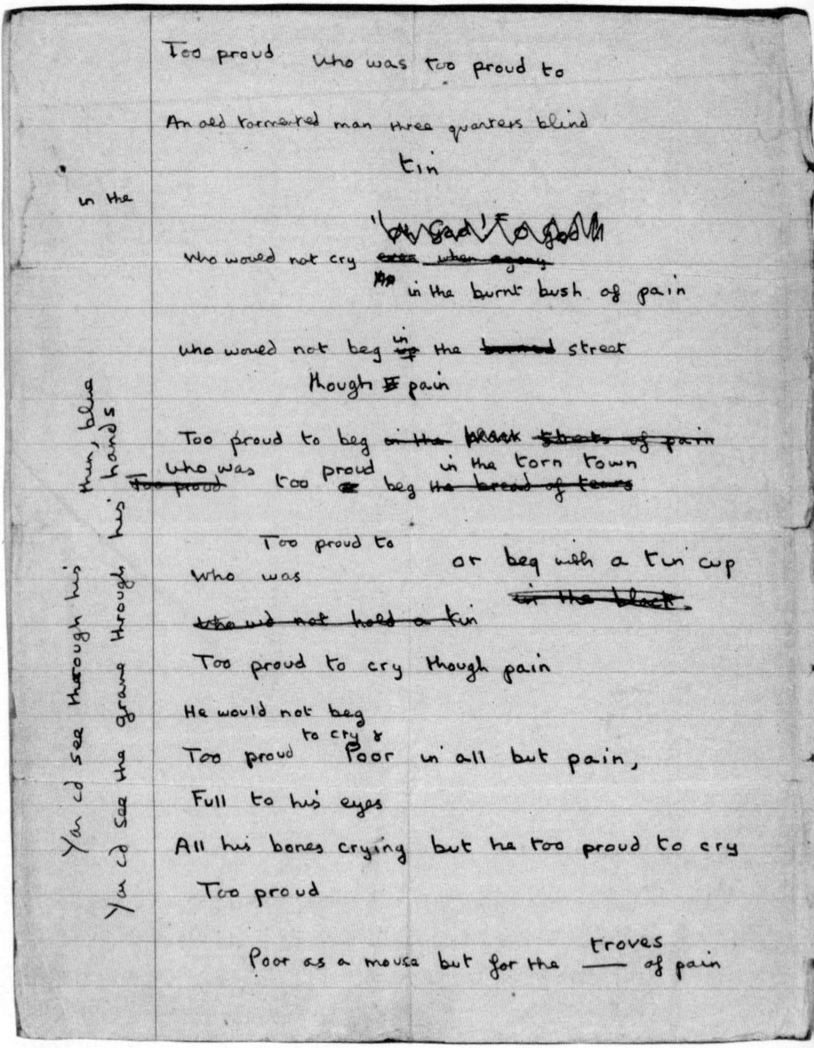

Too proud   Who was too proud to

An old tormented man three quarters blind

tin

in the

~~bread of teeth~~

Who would not cry ~~out when agony~~

in the burnt bush of pain

who would not beg in the ~~burned~~ street

though ~~I~~ pain

Too proud to beg ~~in the~~ ~~black~~ ~~street~~ ~~of pain~~

in the torn town

~~Too proud~~ Who was too ~~to~~ beg ~~the~~ ~~bread of tears~~

Too proud to

Who was   or beg with a tin cup

~~who would not hold a tin~~ ~~in the black~~

Too proud to cry though pain

He would not beg

to cry &

Too proud Poor in all but pain,

Full to his eyes

All his bones crying but he too proud to cry

Too proud

troves

Poor as a mouse but for the ——— of pain

(left margin, vertical):
Hun, blue his hands

Yan cd see through his

Yan cd see the grave through

A draft of 'Elegy' from DT's notebook

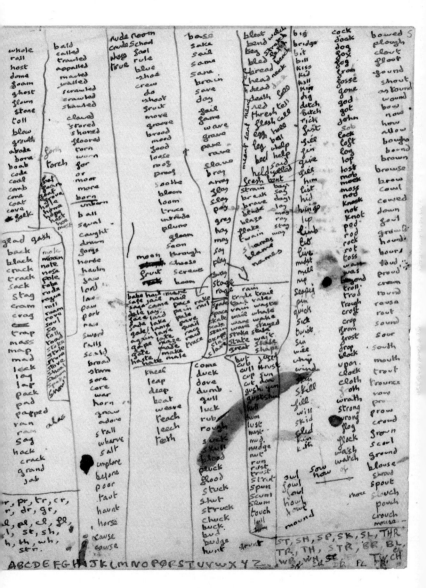

DT's list of rhyming words

I have a lot of
ideas — good, bad,
& chaotic.

The Boat House,
Laugharne,
Carmarthenshire,
Wales.

16 June 1953

Dear ~~Mr~~ Igor Stravinsky,

I was so very very glad
to meet you, for a little time, in Boston;
~~and~~ you and your wife couldn't have been
kinder to me. I hope you get well very
soon.

I haven't heard anything from Sarah Caldwell
yet, but I've been thinking a lot about
~~theatre~~ the opera. ~~And~~ As soon as
I can get something down on paper, I
would love to send it to you. ~~I've only~~
~~just returned home here~~ I broke my
arm just before leaving New York the
week before last, & ~~haven't~~ can't write
properly yet. It was only a little break,
they tell me, but it cracked like a

gun.
I shd like very much — if you think
you wd still like me to work with you;
& I'll be enormously honoured to do
that — to come to California to see you
in late September or early October.
Wd that be convenient? I do hope so.
And by that time, I hope, too, to
have some clearer ideas about a ~~subject~~.

DT's letter to Stravinsky about their plans to co-write
an opera, sent just months before DT's death

Mr Miron Grindea
Editor
ADAM
28 Emperor's Gate
London S.W. 7 (England)

Dear Sir,

Your letter of December 15, 1953, reached me with some delay,
and I am also answering it with delay, due to the fact that
I am currently on a concert tour and travelling all over the
country.

Dylan Thomas' sudden passing away has left me deeply shocked
and painfully wounded. As you know, he was in New York on the
first leg of his journey to my home in California, and we were
both eagerly looking forward to getting better acquainted
personally and working on the idea of an opera.

I met Dylan Thomas only once, and unfortunately much too
briefly, in Boston last May, when he came to my hotel room
to visit me. Immediately I was as much fascinated by his
intelligence, personality, genuine charm, as I had been left
impressed by the reading of his powerful and highly poetical
writings.

Dylan Thomas' hopes and enthusiasm were certainly the same
than mine when he embarked on his ill-fated voyage. He did
not live to let them take shape materially and artistically,
but he left to me, with the strong imprint of his personality,
the great sadness of a beautiful dream which could not be born
to life.

I wish your memorial number of ADAM on Dylan Thomas will be
a so well deserved tribute to him. Among all those who are
better qualified than I am to make the eulogy of this very
great poet -- because they have been privileged to know him
better and longer -- my own tribute must necessarily be short
but it is a most sincere and enthusiastic one, even it has
to be limited to this letter to the Editor of ADAM.

Sincerely,

Igor Stravinsky

Stravinsky's letter to *Adam International Review*'s DT memorial issue

NOTES

(Very) Early Poems

A visit to the house where DT wrote these poems is recommended: 5 Cwmdonkin Drive, Swansea. It's kept as a kind of museum, kitted out as it might have been when Dylan himself lived there.

Head up the stairs and towards the box room. Here, in the tiniest bedroom imaginable, is where he wrote so many of these extraordinary poems, ones which have since travelled the world, given pleasure to so many for so long, and continue doing so.

The first few poems I include were written by Dylan as a child. According to Florence, his mother, he started writing poems when he was very young, not even ten years old. Here's Florence talking to my uncle, Colin Edwards, about those early poems:

'Do you have any of these now?'

'No-o. Well, I tell you what, I put them somewhere, on the mantelpiece I think, the following day, I was tidying up, and I sorted them out. There was one lot I was going to burn, one lot I was going to keep. Well, I burnt the wrong ones. So, of course, I was very disappointed… but you couldn't keep all his stuff he was writing, because—well, I'd have had the house full. We wouldn't have had a room to live in. We never thought he was going to be a poet or anything else in that way.'

'Did they note his talent in school?'

'As regards English, he was always top. But as regards everything else, he didn't bother. And of course, it was so awkward for his dad, being the English master. Do you know, I've seen Daddy looking through his papers when he'd been marking with them at home. He'd be looking through them and he'd try to see some fault, but he couldn't. And then he'd have to give him top marks. He couldn't do otherwise.'

'Mr Thomas, his father, must have given him great encouragement and guidance in his writing.'

'Oh yes, he did, oh yes. When he was very small, I used to say, "Oh Daddy, don't read Shakespeare to a child only about four years of age. He doesn't understand this." And he used to say, "Well, he'll understand it. It'll be just the same as if I was reading an ordinary thing." So he was brought up on Shakespeare. But he did love poems. And of course, Daddy did have a good library of books. A tremendous library.'

'Dylan wasn't a reserved young boy was he?'

'Well, he was reserved in a way. He had to know you first before he would let himself go. No one knew that there was so much humour in him when he was a young lad, only his friends because if he met somebody, he would sort of close up, until he got to know them. Then he would start.'

(From *Dylan Remembered: Vol. I, 1914–1934*, ed. David N. Thomas)

THE SONG OF THE MISCHIEVOUS DOG

The first poem DT ever published, this appeared in the Swansea area only, and was written when he was eleven.

'THE SECOND BEST'

Credited to Dylan Marlais, this appeared in *The Boy's Own Annual*, 1927, making it his first UK-wide published poem. He would have been twelve or thirteen.

Interesting to note, this boy, born in the year in which the First World War erupted, one of the deadliest global conflicts in history, showing early interest and sympathy for the sacrifices and burdens of the common man. In DT's 'Reminiscences of Childhood' (1943) he remembers adults all talking about 'the Front' and how he was puzzled about men not coming back from there because the only front he knew was his front parlour and door.

Dylan would remain left-leaning all his life, and when Henry Treece, in his book *Dylan Thomas: 'Dog Among the Fairies'* (1949), asserted that DT had left the Marxism of his youth behind, adding that Dylan's poems had no social awareness, DT retorted in a letter: 'Surely it is evasive to say my poetry has no social awareness—no evidence of contact with society… actually, "seeking kinship" with everything… is exactly what I do do' (all quotations from DT's letters come from the two *Collected Letters* volumes published by Weidenfeld & Nicholson).

LA DANSEUSE

On the handwritten copy of this poem you can see that another hand has added 'enamoured' above the original 'enarmoured', also against 'epitome' you'll find 'ep/i/to/me—4 syllables'. Again, with another poem: 'Real is two syllables and cannot rhyme with steel.' Presumably all these notes hint at the guiding hand and teachings of his father. I love the image of these two generations, one stood overlooking the other's work.

FOREST PICTURE

From the *Swansea Grammar School Magazine*, March 1928. DT became editor in 1929 and contributed generously—'stories, light verse, parodies of modern poets like Osbert Sitwell, Sassoon and Yeats, an article about Modern Poetry written at 15 and no less than twenty-six poems in six years'. I quote Suzanne Roussillat here, from *Adam International Review* 1953, 'Our Dylan Thomas Memorial Number'.

I've included this poem as it clearly shows his love of nature. 'Summer is heavy with age, and leans upon Autumn.' What a line—boom! The stirrings of a master's voice.

CLOWN IN THE MOON

Written as text to go with his polymath friend Daniel Jones's music, dated 28th April 1929.

> I think, that if I touched the earth,
> > It would crumble;
> It is so sad and beautiful

Here, an early hint at his preoccupation with the precarious, essential dance of life and death.

THE PINE

Written as text to go with Daniel Jones's music, dated 7th May 1929.

Other titles from around this time include 'The Elm', 'The Oak', 'My River', 'Of Any Flower', 'To A Slender Wind'. Nature looms large.

NO, PIGEON, I'M TOO WISE

Dated 8th August 1930, from the notebook held at the State University of New York at Buffalo. DT sold three of his early notebooks to a London antiquarian book dealer, Bertrand Rota, when he was around twenty-six. Rota sold them on to the the library of State University of New York at Buffalo.

> I'm all for ground,
> To touch what's to be touched,
> To imitate myself mechanically,
> Doing my little tricks of speech again

With all my usual care.
No bird for me:
He flies too high.

'Doing my little tricks of speech again': an endearing nod to his love for the effect and sounds of language, and some kind of humbleness too? Certainly a reference to the physicality and labour of writing: the workings, the observations, the savouring. Compare this with his later poem 'In my craft or sullen art'.

Notebook Poems

Before his nineteenth birthday, DT would write around two hundred poems and fill innumerable school exercise books, of which five survive. The fifth turned up relatively recently, out of the blue in 2014, having been languishing in a drawer for decades, the owners unaware of its cultural value.

It was Jeff Towns (aka 'Jeff the Books', or 'The Dylan Thomas Guy', the world's leading DT expert, antiquarian, chairman of the Dylan Thomas Society, previous owner of Dylan's Mobile Bookstore and Dylan's Bookshop) who made the winning bid at Sotheby's on behalf of Swansea University when it was put up for auction. The price with premium was £104,500. (The other four are held by the State University of New York at Buffalo.)

By 1941, DT had sold four of these notebooks to raise money. But their contents would become the wellspring for his first three collections: *18 Poems* (1934), *Twenty-five Poems* (1936) and *The Map of Love* (1939). They reappeared in *Collected Poems 1934–1952*, which contained all works he wanted 'to preserve'.

However, some extraordinary pieces in these notebooks did not gain entry to any of the above. I include them here.

CABARET (OR I, POOR ROMANTIC, HELD HER HEEL)

'I see; / I see the man is mad with love.' I love this dialogue! It reminds me of Mog Edwards from *Under Milk Wood*:

> I am a draper mad with love. I love you more than all the flannelette and calico, candlewick, dimity, crash and merino, tussore, cretonne, crepon, muslin, poplin, ticking and twill in the whole Cloth Hall of the world.

> As that her heel was lifted,
> Gone from my palm to leave it marked
> With quite a kind of heart.
> She is on dancing toes again,
> Sparkling a twelve-legged body
> And many arms to raise
> Over her heel and me.

What wonderful imagery here—a young man infatuated by a girl dancing—we've only just begun, and we already have two poems inspired by a dancer! Dylan would go on to marry one too, Caitlin Macnamara, on 11th July 1937.

They met the year before in a pub, either the Wheatsheaf or the Fitzroy; introduced by the painter Augustus John, the youngsters apparently bonded immediately.

NOTEBOOK 2: 1930–32

BEING BUT MEN, WE WALKED INTO THE TREES

DT celebrates the innocence and wonder of children against the foil of life-weary, fearful and wonder-less older beings.

The poem gives this book its title as, taken simply and out of context of the poem as whole, I've found the line often pops to mind, offering comfort and hope in this complex world.

It also makes me think of writers and creatives and the infinite variables we face: the words, patterns, rhythms, rhymes, made-up words, phrases, reordered phrases, different languages, proverbs and quotes—a universe of choices to plunder, and out of which we hope to birth something special.

It's a good fit, I think, for DT too. The work of the best artists seems effortless, natural even, but DT despaired at the thought that he produced work much as a tap turned, gushed water. Rather, he compared his discipline to the whittler of wood, honing it into shape with patience and time—and for me it is this image of the focused, even obsessed, toiling craftsman that prevails, one who can harness beauty and power from the chaos of his surroundings, his source material.

NOTEBOOK 3: 1933

BEFORE THE GAS FADES

Dated 6th February 1933, written a week after Hitler was sworn in as German Chancellor on 30th January 1933.

This feels like a bitter tirade. Might it be in response to the Great Depression of the 1930s—when the decline of the coal industry in Wales meant that by 1932 nearly half of all men were unemployed? Here also feel the spectre of the march of industry and corporation over the individual and the country's trauma post-First World War; plus the clouds of war are gathering again. It's 1933, Hitler and his Nazi Party are in power, Germany is now a dictatorship.

> Before civilisation rises or rots
> (It's a matter of guts,
> Graft, poison, and bluff,
> Sobstuff, mock reason,

> The chameleon coats of the big bugs and shots),
> The jaws will have shut, and life be switched out.

The poem's energy, its unmasked distaste at man's terrorizing fecklessness, reminds me of a young Bob Dylan. I'm writing this in 2023 witnessing our own 'big shots' and their 'chameleon coats', the rise of the far right and fake news and corruption, AI, earthquakes, floods and fires, the fears around climate change and power-holders in global capitalism. The poem resonates.

'WE WHO WERE YOUNG ARE OLD'

Dated 16th February 1933.

Another poem of despair from the 'prematurely aged' generation who saw a second world war on the horizon, while still living with the realities and after-effects of the first.

I can't help thinking of anti-war songs like 'Johnny I Hardly Knew Ye' [Roud 3137], first published 1867, written by Joseph B. Geoghegan; or 'Green Fields of France', Eric Bogle, 1976), especially around these lines:

> The Piccadilly men* the back street drunks,
> The grafters of cats' heads on chickens' trunks,
> The whole, the crippled, the weak and strong,
> The Western man with one lung gone

OUT OF A WAR OF WITS

Dated 22nd February 1933.

'War' here refers to wars of words and debate, which DT had regularly with his friends, the oft-called Kardomah gang (they met in the Kardomah Café). People like Bert Trick, the 'small-c communist grocer'; Daniel Jones, composer; Vernon Watkins, poet; Alfred Janes,

---

* Night-time frequenters of bars and clubs in Piccadilly.

artist; and Charles Fisher, poet. Topics might have included Picasso, Stravinsky, Einstein...

> It is good that the sun shine,
> And, after it has sunk, the sane moon,
> For out of a house of matchboard and stone
> Where men would argue till the stars be green,
> It is good to step onto the earth, alone,
> And be struck dumb, if only for a time.

I love the image it encourages of a befuddled boffin stepping out blinking from the shadows, from an exhausting session of theorizing, made, for once, to feel absolved and impotent under the infinite, eternal universe.

THAT SANITY BE KEPT

It's been suggested that this might have been torn out of Notebook 3, and if so it dates from around late July or early August 1933.

I adore this—that sober self-awareness, the complexities and machinations of the mind while observing the mundane, the everyday. But what did DT think? This comes from a letter to Pamela Hansford Johnson, his first love, dated September 1933:

> The more I think of my Referee poem the less I like it. The idea of self, sitting in the open window, in my shirt, and imagining myself as some Jehovah of the West, is really odd. If I were some Apollo it would be different.

Would choosing Apollo, god of sun, light and poetry etc., be a more fun, less grandiose comparison? Either way, the act of sitting in a window, pondering the big stuff while observing the humdrum, is one we can easily imagine or identify with.

I also love how we witness DT here processing the scenes and sounds around him as music:

161

The sweet suburban music from a hundred lawns
Comes softly to my ears. The English mowers mow and mow.

Just for fun here, I'm going to admit that these lines always make me think of Joni Mitchell's *The Hissing of Summer Lawns* (1975)—and, if you'll forgive me, 'I Know What I Like (In Your Wardrobe)' by Genesis, from the *Selling England by the Pound* album (1973). If you don't know it, it's a song sung from the perspective of a lawnmower.

FOR AS LONG AS FOREVER IS

Unfinished, *c*.1938.

In *Letters to Vernon Watkins* you read that DT thought the opening line 'completely out of place', which is presumably why he leaves this work unfinished (though the line does reappear in his 'Twenty-four Years').

These lines:

And the fast sky quakes in the web [...]
Shakes in its stride the partridge fence and the sea-duck rows [...]
And the stag through a trap grave,
Forever the hunted world at a snail's gallop goes.

... are just so DT!

From 18 Poems *(1934)*

I SEE THE BOYS OF SUMMER

Notebook 4, poem '39', dated April 1934:

There from their hearts the dogdayed* pulse
Of love and light bursts in their throats.

Again, here we see how DT loves to play with the English language; conjoining words, using them in different ways or even making up

---

* Dog days: hot, sultry weather, or a period marked by dull lack of progress.

words. 'We are the dark deniers'... as in deny-er, 'One who denies',
which is commonplace today.

THE FORCE THAT THROUGH THE GREEN FUSE

Poem '23', dated 12th October 1933, was published in the *Sunday Referee*
on 29th October 1933 and won its best annual poem prize.

This poem has become one of his most lauded. It's been compared to
Wordsworth's 'Tintern Abbey', which Dylan admired for its pantheistic*
creed:

> And I have felt
> A presence that disturbs me with the joy
> Of elevated thoughts; a sense sublime
> Of something far more deeply interfused,
> Whose dwelling is the light of setting suns,
> And the round ocean and the living air,
> And the blue sky, and in the mind of man:
> A motion and a spirit, that impels
> All thinking things, all objects of all thought,
> And rolls through all things.

Which brings me to this question by Professor Brian Cox: 'There is only one
interesting existential question: What does it mean to live a small, finite
life in a possibly infinite, eternal Universe?' And round and round we go.

Another comparison is made by Walford Davies and Ralph Maud,
who in *Collected Poems 1934–1953* cite William Blake's 'The Sick Rose' as a
possible inspiration for DT's poem:

> O Rose thou art sick.
> The invisible worm,
> That flies in the night
> In the howling storm,

---

* Pantheism being the view that the entire natural universe is divine and
so should be revered.

163

Has found out thy bed
Of crimson joy:
And his dark secret love
Does thy life destroy.

And DT does go on to acknowledge Blake's influence in this excerpt from a letter he wrote to his first love, the writer Pamela Hansford Johnson, dated 15th October 1933:

I am in the path of Blake, but so far behind him that only the wings on his heels are in sight. I have been writing since I was a very little boy, and have always been struggling with the same things, with the idea of poetry as a thing entirely removed from such accomplishments as 'word-painting,' and the setting down of delicate but usual emotions in a few, well-chosen words. There must be no compromise; there is always only the one right word: use it, despite its foul or merely ludicrous associations.

WHERE ONCE THE WATERS OF YOUR FACE

Poem '38', dated 18th March 1934.

It's worth reminding ourselves that DT was still a teenager when he wrote these poems. They reveal an adolescent absorbed with mortality, no surprise given that he was born in the year the First World War started, though there are many other factors to consider, including being a youngster in an ageing family.

There's a fascinating article I came across recently by David N. Thomas,* 'Dylan Thomas and his aunties: The other women in the poet's life'. In it he writes:

---

*   David N. Thomas is the author of a number of DT books, including the two volumes of *Dylan Remembered* (2003, 2004), which are edited transcripts of my uncle Colin Edwards's interviews with Dylan's family, friends, teachers and colleagues, as well as *Fatal Neglect: Who Killed Dylan Thomas?* (2008). Well worth reading.

The most striking characteristic of these aunts is their age: the oldest, Annie Fernhill, was in her sixties, and the youngest, Theodosia, in her fifties, when Dylan, a schoolboy, went to stay with them. When, as a teenager, he stayed with Polly at Blaencwm she, too, was in her sixties. To the young Dylan, his aunts must have seemed more like grandmothers. Even his first cousins would have seemed 'old', for they were already in their twenties and thirties when he was a boy, whilst his parents were in their forties.

David goes on to list at least seven family deaths and the funeral of a schoolteacher in 1932, which DT attends, and his father's cancer diagnosis, then he adds:

Tragedy also pressed in from outside. In March 1934, two sisters killed themselves in the Tywi. They were found in the river still in an embrace, each with an arm around the other's neck, their bodies tied together at the waist. A few days later, Dylan was writing 'Where once the waters of your face'.

DT also writes about fertility—and let's note here that no children were born to any of Florence's Llangain relations between 1903 and 1933. The family was at risk, then, of failing to renew itself. Dylan's birth in 1914 made him the first boy born in sixteen years to his close family, and he was, yes, therefore indulged—not only by his mother and older sisters but, as David notes in his article, by his older (female) first cousins too: 'everybody mothered Dylan, everybody, even my family mothered Dylan'.

ESPECIALLY WHEN THE OCTOBER WIND

This is a birthday poem, revised for publication in *The Listener* on 24th October 1934; an early version possibly dates from 1932.

When I experience anything, I experience it as a thing and a word
at the same time, both equally amazing

(DT, quoted in Davies and Maud (eds.),
Collected Poems 1934–1953)

In this poem, Dylan takes our hand and makes us walk in the shoes
of a poet—so as we can witness his lot: his task is to walk the world,
rebuild the essence of its reality with just words. But it's an even bigger
challenge than this—he wishes 'to communicate at a deeper-than-
language level' (John Goodby (ed.), *The Collected Poems of Dylan Thomas*).

LIGHT BREAKS WHERE NO SUN SHINES

Dated 20th November 1933, published in *The Listener*, 14th March 1934.

DT had apparently been watching horror films around this time.
Here's an excerpt from a December 1933 letter to Pamela Hansford
Johnson, which accompanies another poem of the same period ('See,
says the lime', about the hangman's lime used to help break down the
bodies of the executed), sharing a similar ground of growth and decay
and the interrelation of life and death:

> I suppose it's my usual stuff again, and even a little more death-
> struck. But don't be put off by my anatomical imagery, which I
> explained months ago. Because I so often write in terms of the
> body, of the death, disease, and breaking of the body, it doesn't
> necessarily mean that my Muse (*not* one of my favourite words) is
> a sadist. For the time at least, I believe in the writing of poetry from
> the flesh, and generally from the dead flesh

And again, awareness that he tends to return again and again to the
visceral (the following excerpt is from a letter of early January 1934 to
his pal Trevor Hughes):

They are, I admit, unpretty things, with their imagery almost totally anatomical. But I defend the diction, the perhaps wearisome succession of blood and bones, the never ending similes of the streams of veins and the lights in the eyes, by saying that, for the time at least, I realise that it is impossible for me to raise myself to the altitude of the stars, and that I am forced, therefore, to bring down the stars to my own level and to incorporate them into my own physical universe

I want to add one more point of interest before we move on from 'Light breaks'. Jeff Towns is writing a new book about DT, and in it will be a chapter about this very poem. Jeff acquired (from Daniel Jones's archive) DT's ink-stained and scruffy School Physics Exercise Book, labelled 'D. M. Thomas 1VA' on the upper cover. It dates from 1926 and among the rough jottings from a lecture on light, these prescient physics notes are found written in his schoolboy hand:

> Light
> Light is invisible.
> Light travels in straight lines.

(The exercise book is now part of the Jeff Towns/Dylan Thomas Collection at the National Library of Wales.)

I DREAMED MY GENESIS

An early version appears as 'Two' in Notebook 2, and is rewritten in late April/May 1934.

According to one of DT's letters, 'the one beginning "I dreamed my genesis" is more or less based on Welsh rhythms, and may seem, rhythmically, a bit strange at first'. Proof here, then, if we even needed it, of DT's knowledge of Welsh classical poetry and the metrical and musical techniques of Cynghanedd. There's a hint of an 'Englyn', the traditional Cornish and Welsh form of short poetry, here too in the way the phrasings work.

167

Again DT plunders his preoccupations with the cosmos, the elements within it and us, to birth yet another poem on death, rebirth and death, this time partly written from the perspective of the poet himself being born, and partly from that of a mortally wounded soldier dying on the front line during the First World War.

From Twenty-Five Poems *(1936)*

WHY EAST WIND CHILLS

An early version is dated 1st July 1933 and named poem '37'; this version was published on 16th July 1936 in *New English Weekly*.

This makes me think of the 'Why? Why? Why?' questioning by very young children—and in Davies and Maud's edition of DT's poems, they write that a line in the early version was indeed inspired by a little girl aged four asking the wonderful question 'What colour is glory?'. This was subsequently changed by DT to 'When cometh Jack Frost?' in this published version, though the child's original (wonderful) line does turn up later in another poem, 'My World Is Pyramid'.

> Why east wind chills and south wind cools
> Shall not be known till windwell dries
> And west's no longer drowned

These lines also have hints of a Welsh-language children's song called 'Migldi Magldi' (as in the never, never...).

> Pan ddaw'r mor I ben y mynydd,
> A'i ddwy ymyl at ei gilydd,
> A'r coed rhosys yn dwyn fala,
> Dyna'r pryd y cei di finna
>
> When the sea come to the mountain's summit,
> And its edges come together,

And the rose bush reaps apples,
That's when you can have me

THE HAND THAT SIGNED THE PAPER

A notebook version, 'One', is dated 17th August 1933; it was revised and finally published in *New Verse* in December 1935. 'One' was dedicated to A.E.T., DT's political mentor and influential friend Bert Trick. (It was Bert's daughter, Pamela, who asked, 'What colour is glory?'.)

But let's, for now, head back to Henry Treece's *'Dog Among the Fairies'*, which I mentioned earlier. Dylan was not a big fan! Jeff Towns owns two copies of this book, both signed by DT. In one the inscription reads:

I will not sign this book
Dylan Thomas

In the other:

I hate this stinking book but I'll sign it anyway
Dylan Thomas

Treece had commented in the book that 'The hand that signed the paper' was unique among DT's works, it being overtly political—and this provoked a rant from our poet, well worth repeating here:

But the idea you gave me was that you actually consider me unaware of my surroundings, out-of-contact with the society from which I am necessarily outlaw. You are right when you suggest that I think a squirrel stumbling at least of equal importance as Hitler's invasions, murder in Spain, the Garbo-Stokowski romance, royalty, Horlick's, lynchlaw, pit disasters, Joe Louis, wicked capitalists, saintly communists, democracy, the Ashes, the Church of England, birthcontrol, Yeats' voice, the machines of the world I tick and revolve in, pub-baby-weather-government-football-youthandage-

169

speed-lipstick, all small tyrannies, means tests, the fascist anger,
the daily, momentary lightnings, eruptions, farts, dampsquibs,
barrelorgans, tinwhistles, howitzers, tiny death-rattles, volcanic
whimpers of the work I eat, drink, love, work, hate and delight
in—but I *am* aware of these things as well.

(DT letter to Treece, July 1938)

SHOULD LANTERNS SHINE

Published in *New Verse*, December 1935, but probably written at least a
year earlier.

> I have been told to reason by the pulse,
> And, when it quickens, alter the actions' pace
> Till field and roof lie level and the same
> So fast I move defying time

The design of the above section is so enjoyable to read out—it makes
you want to speed up—and mimicks the quickening pulse he refers to
in this poem reflecting on time, ageing, impulses, heart versus head.
The last lines are pretty special too—what a brilliant image!

> The ball I threw while playing in the park
> Has not yet reached the ground.

It's easy to imagine DT as a kind of Peter Pan figure; at the very least,
one quickly understands that keeping a sense of youthful wonder was
important to him. Let's see what his daughter Aeronwy has to say about
this quality, here in a 2009 newspaper article:

> Practically and emotionally, Dylan was a dependent man-baby:
> Caitlin cut his nails, arranged Dolly Mixtures around the edge
> of his bath for him to eat while soaking. 'Myself, I think he was
> in mourning for the state of childhood, when you don't have
> responsibilities,' Aeronwy says, drily.

('Dylan Thomas's daughter: "I still get angry with the
self-destruction of my father"', *Daily Mail*, 15th August 2009)

Aeronwy was ten when her father died. Her memories are more about the writer than the headline-grabbing actor. She remembers standing at the door of his writing shed, listening to him mumbling through his poetry or occasionally shouting it out loud. You can visit the Boat House in Laugharne; peep into his shed, which teeters on the cliff-edge offering a panoramic view of the estuary, and spot photographs of W.H. Auden, Byron and Edward Thomas pinned around his desk.

I HAVE LONGED TO MOVE AWAY

An early version is dated 1st March 1933, St David's Day, when traditionally you'd go to school in the scratchy woollen flannel of Welsh traditional costume, a daffodil or leek pinned to your chest—and girls, you'd be wobbling a tall black hat with white-lace trims badly on your head. Reason enough to want to move away from Wales, even just for brief moments? Especially when we'd all start nibbling at the raw leeks throughout the day.

DT would have been eighteen—just a handful of months away from his first foray to London, a youth eager to move but naturally nervous about change. He would revise the poem a few years later, now a successful and famous writer, and, with the Second World War looming, added edge. DT's reference to the 'old lie' takes us to Wilfred Owen's First World War classic, 'Dulce et Decorum Est': 'The old lie: *Dulce et decorum est | Pro patria mori*'.

Does death's feather also refer to the practice of giving a white feather to those not wearing uniform to try and shame them into signing up to fight during the First World War?

It would eventually be published in *New Verse* in 1935.

GRIEF THIEF OF TIME

The beginnings of this poem date from 1933 in two separate ideas. The revised version emerged as one and was published in *Comment*, February 1936.

171

Read at least this one aloud (as Dylan would suggest, I'm sure). There's such a weight to the sound it makes:

> The old forget the cries,
> Lean time on tide and times the wind stood rough,
> Call back the castaways

A very beautiful poem, rhythm- and voice-wise—I can't help wondering whether DT was inspired to write this, and other poems about death and loss, following his father's cancer diagnosis in summer 1933. DJ had a malignant ulcer under his tongue for which he underwent painful radium treatment. Debilitation forced DJ to retire early, though he lived for another twenty years. He died on 16th December 1952, just eleven months before his son followed him to the grave.

DT was very close to his father. Cancer, the word and the disease itself, seems to hold a fascination for him: 'The root of tongues ends in a spent out cancer' comes from his poem 'From love's first fever'.

'Grief thief of time', in my understanding, touches on the difference between how one deals with death when young, as compared to when older. Death can cause inconceivable shock when first you experience it—that one day a living, breathing person can be here and the next not. I guess there's a gradual acceptance of this as we grow older, not that it ever gets easy to process.

The poem throws up images of wartime losses and grief, time as healer of grief, grief as distorter of time, and the irony of the seeds of new life being present in the body of a dying person.

AND DEATH SHALL HAVE NO DOMINION

An early version was published in *New English Weekly* on 18th May 1933, but it didn't appear in its final form until 2nd June 1936, one of the last poems to be submitted to be part of *Twenty-Five Poems*, published in September 1936.

For some reason, Dylan was hesitant about putting it forward. It was his friend Vernon Watkins who assured him that it needed to be included, as he loved its 'impulsive rhythm'. It was the result of a challenge to write a great poem on immortality, according to Bert Trick.

DT takes inspiration from Romans 6:9, 'Knowing that Christ being raised from the dead dieth no more; death hath no more dominion over him.' But the poem expands the idea of Christ's rebirth and Christian belief in life after death to a more pantheistic view that, after death, our matter in some form or other remains part of the natural cycle and so in theory we remain part of the living world.

I love that there's more potential evidence here of his knowledge of the Welsh language:

> may a flower no more
> Lift its head to the blows of the rain

'Mae hi'n bwrw glaw' in Welsh means it is raining, though literally it means the rain is hitting or striking blows.

From The Map of Love *(1939)*

BECAUSE THE PLEASURE-BIRD WHISTLES

Published in *Twentieth Century Verse*, February 1939. Once entitled 'January 1939', it's a New Year poem. Here's DT himself with more, from a letter to Desmond Hawkins:

> The poem begins with a queer question about a bird and a horse; because one thing is made sweeter (qualify this word) through suffering what it doesn't understand, does that mean everything is sweeter through incomprehensible, or blind, suffering?

Some of the ideas for the poem came to DT in a dream:

> The image of a singing horse came from a dream of Dylan's. In which a horse stood in a cage made of wires which gradually became red-hot, on which a man standing by said, 'he sings better now.'
>
> (Vernon Watkins's notes, from Gwen Watkins's *Portrait of a Friend*)

173

This was the 1930s, a time when the Surrealist movement was bursting out of the avant-garde and into the mainstream, and there are eyebrow-raising stories of Dylan during this time doing rather odd things like going round the pub on his hands and knees, barking, or, aged twenty-one at an international Surrealist conference in London (where Salvador Dalí nearly suffocated in his diving suit) offering people an empty cup with a boiled piece of string in it, asking 'Weak or strong?'

Here's DT again on this work, from the same letter to Hawkins:

> Later the poem has a figure in it standing suffering on the tip of the new year and refusing, blindly, to look back at, if you like, the *lessons* of the past year to help him; and the case, which is really a case for a prayer, begins to make itself clear.

I can't help but wonder at this strange pre-feast grace—pertinent as it is—given that this was New Year 1938, with fascism in full swagger, monumental political decisions and agreements being made, and here we stand with the poem saying grace at perhaps an opulent, indulgent feast on the cusp of the Second World War.

WE LYING BY SEASAND

Notebook poem '29', dated 16th May 1933.

I'm led to the wild coasts of West Wales through reading this, it takes me to the edge of land and sea, feeling small, fleeting in the big scheme of things, vulnerable and awestruck by the sky and the changing light on the rocky cliff face.

AFTER THE FUNERAL

The poem that appeared as '6' in a notebook dated 10th February 1933 is the precursor to this final version, which was finished in early 1938 and published a few months later in *Life and Letters Today*, summer 1938.

The listing of what he observes (at the post-funeral gathering) is an aspect of DT's writing that you see so well later in Bob Dylan's work. It's effective! You're there immediately watching from the perspective of this boy alone within a stifling, perplexing scene. The love is palpable, as is his shock: the taxidermy, the dusty plant, Ann's 'sculptured [...] stone' dead body all contrast so vividly with the vitality and life force of the once-living person. More so that this gathering concerns Annie Fernhill, whom he associates so closely with her bountiful farm, itself snug within the bosom of so much nature and more life. You hear his hopeless beseeching, willing the essence of Ann herself, and not conformity, to come true to the rescue.

> call all
> The seas to service that her wood-tongued virtue
> Babble like a bellbuoy over the hymning heads,
> Bow down the walls of the ferned and foxy woods
> That her love sing and swing through a brown chapel

I love this DT quote about his Aunt Annie Fernhill: 'she loved me quite inordinately... petted, patted and spoiled me' (from David N. Thomas, 'Dylan Thomas and his aunties').

And one more thing: according to Vernon Watkins, the phrase 'twitch and cry Love' was inspired by a passage in Djuna Barnes's *Nightwood* (1936), one of DT's favourite books: 'If one gave birth to a heart on a plate, it would say "Love" and twitch like the lopped leg of a frog' (Gwen Watkins, *Portrait of a Friend*).

ONCE IT WAS THE COLOUR OF SAYING

Published in *Wales*, March 1939.

It's interesting to compare the scene here with the one we feel in a later classic by DT, 'The hunchback in the park'. 'Mitching' means playing truant.

An early version from 9th December 1930 was entitled 'How shall the animal'. The later finished version, 'How shall my animal', was published in the *New Directions* annual and *Criterion* in 1938.

The thunder and celebration of sound and alliteration we come to associate so well with DT are abundant here. Try this:

> The black, burst sea rejoice,
> The bowels turn turtle,
> Claw of the crabbed veins squeeze from each red particle
> The parched and raging voice?

And again, these first lines from the fourth verse:

> Sigh long, clay cold, lie shorn,
> Cast high, stunned on gilled stone; sly scissors ground in frost
> Clack through the thicket of strength

He admitted that he'd had to work on this poem for months, and it's another example of his embrace of all aspects of life as subject matter for his poems—decomposition, blood, guts, our inner workings...

There's an interesting DT quote from a letter dated 1933 which touches on this (a continuation of the quote I included with the poem 'Light breaks where no sun shines'):

> So many poets take the *living* flesh as their object, and, by their clever dissecting, turn it into a carcass. I prefer to take the *dead* flesh, and, by any positivity of faith and belief that is in me, build up a living flesh from it.

As to the larger aim of the poem, here's a revealing paragraph about just that, from a letter DT wrote to Henry Treece, dated 16th May 1938:

> I hold a beast, an angel and a madman in me, and my enquiry is as to their working, and my problem is their subjugation and victory,

downthrow & upheaval, and my effort is their self-expression. The new poem I enclose, 'How Shall My Animal', is a detailed enquiry; and the poem too is the result of the enquiry, and is the furthest I can, at present, reach or hope for. The poem is, as all poems are, its own question and answer, its own contradiction, its own agreement. I ask only that my poetry should be taken literally. The aim of a poem is the mark that the poem itself makes; it's the bullet and the bullseye; the knife, the growth, and the patient. A poem only moves towards its own end, which is the last line.

THE TOMBSTONE TOLD

An early version dates from July 1933, and the final version appeared in several different publications in 1938 and 1939.

It's interesting to see which subjects inspire DT to write a poem—in this case it hinges on a tragic love story, where a bride dies while still wearing her wedding dress. The wedding has taken place, but the marriage hasn't been consummated—and the lass is buried under her maiden name *and* her married name.

You can easily imagine the poem being told as a kind of ghost story at night. And it very much reminds me of the story of Nant Gwrtheyrn, in which another young girl dies in her wedding dress. Here's the plot in a nutshell: Meinir, bride-to-be, runs to the hills and hides on the morning of her wedding. As was traditional, the groom and his friends go to find her in order for the ceremony to begin. They don't find her, even after frantic searching. The wedding doesn't take place. After many months, looking high and low, Rhys, on a stormy night, takes shelter under their favourite oak tree. Lightning strikes, cleaving the trunk in half, revealing the dead body of poor Meinir, still in her wedding dress.

Here's DT referring to the end of 'The tombstone told' in a letter to Vernon Watkins, 1938:

I want the girl's *terrible* reaction to orgiastic death to be suddenly altered into a kind of despairing love. As I see it now, it strikes me as very moving, but it may be too much of a shock, a bathetic shock perhaps, and I'd very much like to know what you think.

A SAINT ABOUT TO FALL

Written at the end of 1938 and published in *Poetry*, February 1939.

DT and Caitlin's first child, Llewelyn Edouard Thomas, was born on 30th January 1939. In a letter to Vernon Watkins, DT wrote: 'Remember this is a poem written to a child about to be born… and telling it what a world it will see, what horrors and hells.' And from another letter, dated 14th August 1939:

> All the heavenly business I use because it makes a famous and noble landscape from which to plunge this figure onto the bloody, war-barbed etc earth. It's a poem written on the birth of my son. He was a saint for the poem's sake (hear the beast howl).

IF MY HEAD HURT A HAIR'S FOOT

Published in *Poetry (London)*, April 1939.

Here's DT's introduction before reading this poem on the BBC, which can also be found in his *Quite Early One Morning*:

> The next poem tells of a mother and her child who is about to be born. It is not a narrative, nor an argument, but a series of conflicting images which move through pity and violence to an unreconciled acceptance of suffering: the mothers, *and* the child's. The poem has been called obscure. I refuse to believe that it is obscurer than pity, violence, or suffering. But being poem, not a lifetime, it is more compressed.

Published in *Life and Letters Today*, December 1938.

A birthday poem. I find it fascinating to read DT's discussions with Vernon Watkins about the lines one or other or both receive as weak. In this case, they discourse on 'Bury the dead for fear that they walk to the grave in labour' and worry it echoes Shakespeare too much. But I love it for that.

It's fascinating to read about these to-and-fro amendments. Quite often I find that I prefer the early drafts... but regardless, it goes to show that art can have the potential to always be in flux, much like life itself.

From Deaths and Entrances *(1946)*

THE CONVERSATION OF PRAYERS

Published in *Life and Letters Today*, July 1945, and *New Republic*, 16th July 1945.

Such a strong image and point of view—focusing in on night-time, bedtime prayers and comparing and playing with the hopes and fears of the very young and the very old. One of which will be revisited in *Under Milk Wood*:

OLD MAN
I want my pipe and he wants his bottle.

And again:

FIRST VOICE
Dusk is drowned for ever until to-morrow, It is all at once night now [...]
All over the calling dark, babies and old men are bribed and lullabied to sleep.

179

FIRST WOMAN'S VOICE
Hushabye, baby, the sandman is coming...

SECOND WOMAN'S VOICE (Singing)
Rockabye, grandpa, in the tree top,
When the wind blows the cradle will rock,
When the bough breaks the cradle will fall,
Down will come grandpa, whiskers and all.

POEM IN OCTOBER

Summer 1944 saw a start on this being made, though according to
Vernon Watkins a previous version was possibly started as early as
1938. It was published in *Horizon*, February 1945, and *Poetry* (Chicago),
February 1945.

DT takes our hand and takes us on a walk with him into an all-
encompassing, rolling, ever-changing world of wonder. I love how
nebulous the border seems to be between actuality and his ponderings.

Here's DT discussing the poem in a pair of letters to Watkins: 'A
Laugharne poem: the first place poem I've written'; 'a month & a bit
premature (for my birthday). I do hope you'll like it & wd like very
much to read it aloud to you... It's got, I think, a lovely slow lyrical
movement.'

THIS SIDE OF THE TRUTH

Published in *New Republic*, 2nd July 1945, and in *Life and Letters Today*, July
1945.

Dylan's first child, Llewelyn, was born at the outbreak of the Second
World War. This is a poem about the innocence of youth, in high contrast
to the horrors of the war. Trying to navigate through the fact that,
as John Goodby puts it in his note in DT's *Collected Poems*: '"good and
bad", innocence and guilt, are human concepts, projected on a morally

neutral universe', and hoping too that being unjudging 'amounts to acceptance, and therefore to a paradoxical "love"'. Whichever way we cut it, DT's considerations are plump with the love and tenderness of father for son:

> Like the sun's tears,
> Like the moon's seed, rubbish
> And fire, the flying rant
> Of the sky, king of your six years

LOVE IN THE ASYLUM

Published in the May–June 1941 issue of *Poetry (London)*.

A marriage poem—and what strikes me here is how DT has managed to imbue a poem with the boundless energy of Caitlin Macnamara. I can almost feel the movement of air as she swishes into the room, a sense of her limbs moving, her turbulence, her charisma and life force... and the resulting bewilderment of DT:

> [...] Yet she walks the dust
> > Yet raves at her will
> On the madhouse boards worn thin by my walking tears.

THE HUNCHBACK IN THE PARK

Published in *Life and Letters Today*, October 1941. An early version is found in a notebook poem dated 9th May 1932.

Cwmdonkin Park, with its grass, pavilion, benches and flower beds, is still there, feeling and looking very much like the park in this poem. But somehow it paints a stiller picture—it almost feels two-dimensional against the world conjured here in words. I'm led to compare this poem to the work of artist Claude Monet, founder of Impressionism, with its shifting nature, tempo changes and play with perspective, emotions and imagination.

181

DEATHS AND ENTRANCES

Published in *Horizon*, January 1941.

DT experienced the first air raid in London in the September of 1940, and it haunted him: 'I get nightmares like invasions, all successful' (letter to Vernon Watkins). This is the resulting poem about the event.

The title would be used for his next poetry book, 'because that is all I ever write about or want to write about' (DT, from Gwen Watkins's *Portrait of a Friend*).

ON A WEDDING ANNIVERSARY

A version was published in *Poetry (London)* on 15th January 1941, and the revised version for *Deaths and Entrances* is dated 18th September 1941.

Caitlin and Dylan celebrated three years of marriage on 11th July 1940. Here we have a picture of marriage during a time of war.

ON THE MARRIAGE OF A VIRGIN

An earlier version of this poem is titled 'Sixteen', and dated 22nd March 1933 in a notebook.

This could well have been started as a kind of prothalamion to celebrate the engagement of his sister Nancy, who was married on 27th May 1933. It was revised and dated January 1941 and published in *Life and Letters Today* in October 1945.

IN MY CRAFT OR SULLEN ART

Published in *Life and Letters Today*, October 1945.

Is this a glimpse of DT's inner voice, or sanctum? The wordsmith lost in that strange but privileged place occasionally found, when writing and reading, the total absorption, pin-sharp focus, the one urge, the true aim, all ego lost to this nether-world, devoid of contradictions and contrariness.

CEREMONY AFTER A FIRE RAID

Published in *Our Time*, May 1944.

Isn't it a different kind of reportage to read these poems, written in the middle of the Second World War? At this point, DT and his family had had to move out of London and away from the heavy bombing.

This poem is an astounding assault on our senses, right from the start:

> Myselves
> The grievers
> Grieve
> Among the street burned to tireless death
> A child of a few hours
> With its kneading mouth
> Charred on the black breast of the grave
> The mother dug, and its arms full of fires.

Later, I hear the echo of The Lord's Prayer, and the questioning of it all, of faith, until the poem erupts in the third section, the mute out of the trumpet now, using the repetition of sermon and song to move from despair to sonorous invocation:

> The masses of the infant-bearing sea
> Erupt, fountain, and enter to utter for ever
> Glory glory glory
> The sundering ultimate kingdom of genesis' thunder.

ONCE BELOW A TIME

Published in *Life and Letters Today*, March 1940, and appeared in *New Poems* (1943) and *Selected Writings of Dylan Thomas* (1946).

I imagine DT chuckling when he reads this. Think of the 'Suit you, Sir' sketches from *The Fast Show* (1994–97) then read this:

> Then, bushily swanked in bear wig and tails,
> Hopping hot leaved and feathered
> From kangaroo foot of the earth,
> From the chill, silent centre
> Trailing the frost bitten cloth,
> Up through the lubber crust of Wales
> I rocketed to astonish
> The flashing needle rock of squatters,
> The criers of Shabby and Shorten,[*]
> The famous stitch droppers.

Here DT is looking back, much as he does in the BBC broadcast *Return Journey*, where he describes himself as 'a bit of a shower-off; plus fours and no breakfast, you know'.

DT is putting his contradictory elements on show—the ebullience of the ham, the fashion awareness of the dandy and the self-consciousness of someone with provincial roots navigating a capital city. Essentially, he is the flawed adventurer, cue the references to Columbus and Nansen:

> Combing with antlers, Columbus on fire,
> I was pierced by the idol tailor's eyes,
> Glared through shark mask and navigating head,
> Cold Nansen's beak on a boat full of gongs,
>
> To the boy of common thread,
> The bright pretender, the ridiculous sea dandy…
>
> Lie down, lie down and live
> As quiet as a bone.

So, after all the swish and bluster, the voice urges him to tone it down, to lie low, to paint a picture of stillness. I can't help wondering, as it's wartime and DT wasn't in active service, that perhaps he felt pressure

---

[*]   Haberdashers.

to keep a low profile (he'd been deemed unfit at an army medical at Llandeilo and spent the war years writing scripts for propaganda films for the Ministry of Information).

'Once below a time' is a phrase we'll see again, in 'Fern Hill':

> And once below a time I lordly had the trees and leaves
> > Trail with daisies and barley
> > Down the rivers of the windfall light.

WHEN I WOKE

Published in the autumn 1939 issue of *Seven*, but DT had been carrying this rhyme around for a while—'You woke and the dawn spoke' is in the notebook poem 'Fifty One' from August 1933.

A radio bulletin on 3rd September 1939 announcing the outbreak of the Second World War cuts across Laugharne's day-to-day life— everything is now changed:

> I heard, this morning, waking,
> Crossly out of the town noises
> A voice in the erected air,
> No prophet-progeny of mine,
> Cry my sea town was breaking.
> No Time, spoke the clocks, no God, rang the bells,
> I drew the white sheet over the islands
> And the coins on my eyelids sang like shells.

In a letter to Vernon Watkins dated 25th August 1939, DT wrote: 'This war, trembling even on the edge of Laugharne, fills me with such horror and terror and lassitude.' Four days later, he would write the following to his father:

> It is terrible to have built, out of nothing, a complete happiness— from no money, no possessions, no material hopes—and a way of living, and then to see the immediate possibility of its being exploded and ruined.

AMONG THOSE KILLED IN THE DAWN RAID WAS A MAN AGED A HUNDRED

Published in August 1941 in *Life and Letters Today*.

According to Charles de Lautour, this was inspired by a newspaper article:

> I remember we were both very taken up with this story of the old man, and talked wildly about it, the script forgotten. After a while Dylan turned over the script and on the back of the page wrote down words, changed them, crossed out and re-wrote. In a very short time he took a clean sheet and, using the incredible short stub of pencil he always wrote with whenever at least I saw him writing or he was working with me, wrote out complete the enclosed poem and gave it to me.

This statement accompanies the manuscript of this poem in the Harry Ransom Center, Texas. Both men were working on location for Strand Films in Bradford when they saw the account of an air raid death in Hull. The title was taken from the newspaper headline.

LIE STILL, SLEEP BECALMED

Published in *Life and Letters Today*, June 1945.

There is an earlier draft dated 1944, sent from Sussex (where DT and his family had moved to be away from the resumed air attacks, known as the 'Little Blitz').

Do check out a reading by Richard Burton of this poem. I have to repeat this line too, for the sheer brilliance of its sound: 'We heard the sea sound sing, we saw the salt sheet tell.'

The epicness, and the predicament of man lost at sea brings to mind Coleridge's *The Rime of the Ancient Mariner*:

> The voices of all the drowned swam on the wind.

Open a pathway through the slow sad sail,
Throw wide to the wind the gates of the wandering boat

There is an earlier version, which I include below. Reports and photographs of wounds during the war might have reminded DT of his father's cancer, and the pain he suffered. (DT told Trevor Hughes that his father had been 'operated on for cancer of the throat', and this has become the story most people know.)

The earlier version:

Lie still, you must sleep, sufferer with the wound
In the throat, burning and turning. All night afloat
On the silent sea we have heard the sound
That came from your wound. Your wound is a throat.
Under the mile off moon we trembled listening
To music pouring like blood from the loud wound
And when the bandages broke in a burst of singing
It was to us the music of all the drowned.

Open a pathway through the sails, open
Wide the gates of the wandering boat
For my journey to the end of my wound.
The voices cried when the bandages were broken.
Lie still, you must sleep, hide the night from your throat,
Or we shall obey, and ride with you through the drowned.

VISION AND PRAYER

Published in *Horizon*, January 1945, and *Sewanee Review*, summer 1945.

This is a long poem, with sculpted shapes: the verses in the first part, 'Vision', take the form of rhombuses and in the second part the verses appear as straight-sided hourglasses.

Here's DT after receiving a reaction from Vernon Watkins to a version he sent in August 1944:

> I am so glad you liked the 'Vision & Prayer' poem; and that the diamond shape of the first part seems no longer to you to be cramped & artificed. I agree that the second part is, formally, less inevitable, but I cannot alter it, except, perhaps, I detail…

DT didn't finish this long poem until the promise of peace was on the horizon. He wrote it for his son Llewelyn, though by now he and Caitlin had welcomed their second child, Aeronwy, to the world. She was born on 3rd March 1943 in London. 'Vision and Prayer' presents a strong image of a nervous dad waiting in the room while next door the extraordinary/bloody/smelly/noisy action of birthing takes place. Into the lines seep criticisms of the society into which the baby is being born.

But there are beautiful lines, like this:

> I shall run lost in sudden
> Terror and shining from
> The once hooded room
> Crying in vain
> In the caldron
> of his kiss

There are nods to the Bible—'For I was lost who have come / To dumbfounding haven'—and mention of 'upright Adam'.

Then comes part two, and the three prayers: 'In the name of the lost […] I pray'; 'In the name of the fatherless / In the name of the unborn'. And again:

> In the name of the damned
> I would turn back and run
> To the hidden land
> But the loud sun
> Christens down
> The sky.

I love the questions John Goodby asks in his notes to DT's *Collected Poems*: 'To what extent is the child Christ simply the Christlike potential in all humans (and thus identifiable with Thomas' son/sun LLewelyn)? Does "blinding / One" have the meaning of the "oneness", as of the cosmic unity underlying the process poetic?'

We'll never be 100 per cent sure. Over to DT and the last few words of the poem:

> My voice burns in his hand.
> Now I am lost in the blinding
> One. The sun roars at the prayer's end.

FERN HILL

Published in *Horizon*, October 1945.

The last poem written for his *Deaths and Entrances* collection, this was composed during a summer visit to Carmarthen in 1945, after the end of the war, and DT was keen to include it, as we can see from a letter to his publisher, Dent's:

> I am enclosing a further poem, 'Fern Hill', not so far included in the book, which I very much *want* included as it is an *essential* part of the feeling and meaning of the book as a whole.

It would become one of his big hitters, beloved of many, including our present king. DT calls it both a 'joyful' poem and a poem for 'evenings and tears'. In John Goodby's words, it's a poem 'not just about how it feels to be young but how it feels to *have been* young... it can... be read as a six-day creation poem in which the alternation of day and night is central, the sun appearing in every stanza' (*The Collected Poems of Dylan Thomas*).

Of course, you're welcome to dive deep into the structure and methods DT uses here—or, alternatively, sink back into a mossy lawn and let it tickle your senses as you watch the clouds drift by.

I've set many of these poems (and *A Child's Christmas in Wales*) to music (*Poems and Tiger Eggs*, with Mason Neely). Setting this one in particular was such a joy—we used triplets on a mandolin to evoke the lightness and movement of young imagination and all the shifting scenes which unfold.

Like *Under Milk Wood* and *A Child's Christmas in Wales*, 'Fern Hill' rewards you more with each visit. (Fern Hill was the farm of his Auntie Annie Jones, subject of 'After the Funeral'.)

From In Country Sleep *(1952)*

IN COUNTRY SLEEP

A long poem DT declared almost finished on 11th July 1947 in a letter (from Italy, where he had settled) to his agent, David Higham:

> My poem, of 100 lines, is finished, but needs a few days' work on it, especially on one verse. Then I'll send you a copy. The manuscript is thousands and thousands of foolscap pages scattered all over the place but mostly in the boiler fire. What I'll have to send you will be a fair copy. I think it's a good poem. But it has taken so long, nearly three months to write, that it may be stilted. I hope not.

A version with two sections was published in *The Atlantic* in December 1947 (and *Horizon*, with several misprints). He had planned a third part.

There have been many attempts at explaining the work, and at interpreting who or what exactly is the 'Thief' who threatens the speaker of the poem who, because of said Thief, needs reassuring. Could the Thief be Time? Death? Jealousy? Is this a poem addressed to his daughter? Or his wife, Caitlin, which is what DT told an admirer of 'In Country Sleep'?

There are further options: to a reporter, DT said: 'Alcohol is the thief today. But tomorrow he could be fame or success or exaggerated introspection or self-analysis. The thief is anything that robs you of your faith, of your reason for being' (quoted in Paul Ferris, *Dylan Thomas* (2006)).

It's like 'Fern Hill' turned on its head—as there's a menace about in the countryside now. You feel a heavy despair. This is the fairy tale taking a dark turn:

> As the rain falls, hail on the fleece, as the vale mist rides
> Through the haygold stalls, as the dew falls on the wind-
> Milled dust of the apple tree and the pounded islands
> Of the morning leaves, as the star falls, as the winged
> > Apple seed glides,
> And falls, and flowers in the yawning wound at our sides,
> As the world falls, silent as the cyclone of silence.

Lastly, I include here DT's paraphrasing in prose of the last passage—found in a manuscript in the Harry Ransom Center, Texas:

> If you believe (and fear) that every night, night without end, the Thief comes to try to steal your faith that every night he comes to steal your faith that your faith is there—then you will wake with your faith steadfast and deathless.

OVER SIR JOHN'S HILL

DT started writing this when living at the Boat House in Laugharne in 1949. It was published in the *Hudson Review*, autumn 1950, and *The Times Literary Supplement*, 24th August 1951.

DT returns to a subject over which he obsesses—the cycle of life and death and the cosmos. Here we find another fine example and imagine the poet, in his shed, with that panoramic view of water and sky, observing all life and death before him.

And, on a completely different note, how musical is this end?

> The heron, ankling the scaly
> Lowlands of the waves,
> Makes all the music; and I who hear the tune of the slow,
> Wear-willow river, grave,

Before the lunge of the night, the notes on this time-shaken
Stone for the sake of the souls of the slain birds sailing.

POEM ON HIS BIRTHDAY

This poem was started for DT's thirty-fifth birthday in October 1945, but finished in 1951. It was published in *World Review*, October 1951. A longer version would later be published.

DT said in a letter to Princess Caetani, editor of the journal *Botteghe Oscure*: 'I like it better than anything I have done for a very long time.'

Again his fascination with our mortality—here reaching half his 'Bible span'—asking why we should praise God and the beauty of the world, as we move to a horrible death. Also, for context: America dropped the atomic bomb on Hiroshima and Nagasaki on 6th and 9th August 1945 respectively.

> Thirty-five bells sing struck
> On skull and scar where his loves lie wrecked,
> Steered by the falling stars.
> And tomorrow weeps in a blind cage
> Terror will rage apart
> Before chains break to a hammer flame
> And love unbolts the dark

DO NOT GO GENTLE INTO THAT GOOD NIGHT

Published in the journal *Botteghe Oscure* in November 1951.

This was submitted with a covering note: 'I have just finished the short poem I enclose... The only person I can't show the little enclosed poem to is, of course, my father, who doesn't know he's dying.' DT's father died on 16th December 1952.

DT read the poem at the University of Utah in April 1952, and reportedly he began to talk in a soft voice about his father, who, he said, had been a militant atheist, whose atheism had nothing to do with whether there was a God or not, but was a violent and personal dislike for God. He would glare out of the window and growl: 'It's raining, blast Him!' or 'The sun is shining—Lord, what foolishness!' He went blind and was very ill before he died. He was in his eighties, and he grew soft and gentle at the last. Thomas hadn't wanted him to change...

(Davies and Maud (eds.), Collected Poems 1934–1953)

Last Poems

IN COUNTRY HEAVEN

An incomplete draft of forty-three lines was written in March/April 1947. I include DT's reworked sixteen lines, from a notebook dated October 1951.

As Davies and Maud write, 'even incomplete, this first part has accomplished what the poet intended for the whole: it has become an affirmation of the worth of the Earth, "beautiful and terrible"' (*Collected Poems 1934–1953*).

ELEGY

DT was working on this up to a month before he died in November 1953.

There are eighteen pages in a notebook in the Harry Ransom Center in Texas which contain ideas for this poem, as well as thirty-three numbered sheets, and two other worksheets elsewhere. Vernon Watkins has used these workings to offer a longer-form poem, but I'd like to include here the nineteen lines taken to be DT's most finished version. How the quiet and calm contrasts with the commands of 'Do not go gentle'!

There are many ways to skin a cat. (What a strange saying that is.)

It's the last line, 'The air that drew away from him', that strikes me—does it refer to the terrible stillness about a dead body when life has just left it? I do need to add here that DT had crossed out the last two lines in his draft.

PROLOGUE

This was the Prologue to DT's *Collected Poems* (1953), written March–September 1952. Published in *The Listener*, 6th November 1952.

This might be the last finished poem DT wrote. And, as such, I hope its position here, almost at the end of the collection, is understandable, instead of at the beginning, where it is often found.

It's so much fun with this poem to pick out words DT returns to again and again across his writing: cockles, sails, crow black, sunset, clouds, boys, herons, shells, waters, towers, religion, wind, straw, fire, birds, wood, leaves, trees, salmon, swans, dusk... etc! And to question why, given the pressure of delivering an ordinary prose Preface to his *Collected Poems*, he was driven to give himself an extraordinarily technical challenge instead. Here's DT in a letter to his agent David Higham, dated 28th June 1952, letting him know that he was writing

> a Prologue in verse: not dense, elliptical verse, but (fairly) straightforward and colloquial, addressed to the (maybe) readers of the Collected Poems, & full (I hope) of references to my methods of work, my aims, & the kind of poetry I want to write.

At this point he adds that he had written about eighty lines of the 160–200 he aimed to achieve. He went on to finish the Prologue and sent it on 10th September to his editor at Dent's, adding:

I set myself, foolishly perhaps, a most technically difficult task: The Prologue is in two verses... of 51 lines each. And the second verse rhymes *backward* with the first. The first & last lines of the poem rhyme: the second and the last but one; & so on & so on. Why I acrosticked myself like this, don't ask me.

I hope the Prologue *does* read as a prologue, & not just as another poem.

A Final Prayer

REVEREND ELI JENKINS' PRAYER
(FROM *UNDER MILK WOOD*)

> Every morning when I wake,
> Dear Lord, a little prayer I make,
> O please to keep Thy lovely eye
> On all poor creatures born to die

This is more than a poem or a prayer—it is also a hymn that can be sung. The melody is a chant by Arthur Henry Dyke Troyte (1811–57), composer of chants and tunes for the 1857 *Salisbury Hymn Book* in Ireland and the United Kingdom. I sing it often, and was driven to write a new melody for the third verse, 'We are not wholly bad or good', as a kind of bridge section, before ending as per tradition with Troyte's chant and verse four to end.

There's a comfort here, an acceptance of our mortality, while grasping on to life while we have it. It's also reminiscent of an old children's prayer. Compare the following verse:

> And every evening at sun-down
> I ask a blessing on the town,
> For whether we last the night or no
> I'm sure is always touch-and-go.

With this:

> Now I lay me down to sleep,
> I pray the Lord my soul to keep;
> If I should die before I wake,
> I pray the Lord my soul to take.

The poem comes to us via *Under Milk Wood*, DT's play for voices, sung by the Reverend Eli Jenkins as an evening or sunset prayer to the residents now turning down their rooms, drawing curtains, pulling blinds, prepping for night-time.

By following twenty-four hours in the lives of the inhabitants of the backwater seaside town of Llareggub, DT underlines the ebb and flow of life—the rise and fall of the sun and moon, day and night, life and death.

DT came up with ideas that would become *Under Milk Wood* while still at school—and, famously, he was still working on it before curtain-up on the debut performance on 14th May 1953 at 92NY's Kaufmann Concert Hall.

DT read a number of roles that night, including First Voice and, yes, our Reverend Eli Jenkins. It's sad to think that just six months later DT would be lying dead in a New York Hospital bed.

I often wonder what he would have gone on to achieve—the opera he and Stravinsky were cooking up, for example. But here we are, seventy-plus years on, and his distinct writing voice and literary legacy continue to enthral.

In 2023 I pulled together an illustrated children's edition of *Under Milk Wood* with artist Kate Evans and publishers Weidenfeld & Nicolson using DT's original text—a gateway for the very young to enjoy *Under Milk Wood* with no one knowingly left out now!

I'll leave you with another quote attributed to DT: 'Somebody's boring me. I think it's me.'

So, I'll wind things up here. I hope you've enjoyed this collection; I've certainly relished spending time in this world.

Selected Bibliography

Adam International Review: Our Dylan Thomas Memorial Number (No. 238, 1953)

Edwards, Colin, *Dylan Remembered Volume One: 1914–1934*, ed. David N. Thomas (Seren Books, 2003)

———— *Dylan Remembered Volume Two: 1935–1953*, ed. David N. Thomas (Seren Books, 2004)

Ferris, Paul, *Dylan Thomas: The Biography* (Y Lolfa, 2006)

FitzGibbon, Constantine, *The Life of Dylan Thomas* (J.M. Dent & Sons, 1966)

Jones, Daniel, *My Friend Dylan Thomas* (J.M. Dent & Sons, 1977)

Miles, K.G. and Jeff Towns, *Bob Dylan and Dylan Thomas: The Two Dylans* (McNidder & Grace, 2022)

Minhinnick, Robert, *The Mythic Death of Dylan Thomas* (HappenStance, 2014)

Sinclair, Andrew, *Dylan the Bard: A Life of Dylan Thomas* (Constable, 1999)

Thomas, Caitlin with George Tremlett, *Caitlin: A Warring Absence* (Macmillan, 1987)

Thomas, Davin N., 'Dylan Thomas and his aunties: the other women in the poet's life', 2011. https://sites.google.com/site/dylanthomasandhisaunties/dylan-and-his-aunties-a-portrait-of-the-poet-as-an-only-child Accessed December 2023

———— *Fatal Neglect: Who Killed Dylan Thomas?* (Seren Books, 2008)

Thomas, Dylan, *A Child's Christmas in Wales*, illustrated by Edward Ardizzone (Orion, 2006)

———— *The Collected Letters Volume 1: 1931–1939*, ed. Paul Ferris (Weidenfeld & Nicolson, 2017)

———— *The Collected Letters Volume 2: 1939–1953*, ed. Paul Ferris (Weidenfeld & Nicolson, 2017)

———— *The Collected Poems of Dylan Thomas*, ed. John Goodby (Weidenfeld & Nicolson, 2014)

———— *Collected Poems 1934–1953*, ed. Walford Davies and Ralph Maud (J.M. Dent & Sons, 1988)

———— *Letters to Vernon Watkins*, ed. Vernon Watkins (J.M. Dent & Sons, 1957)

———— *A Pearl of Great Price: The Love Letters of Dylan Thomas to Pearl Kazin*, ed. Jeff Towns (Parthian Books, 2013)

———— *The Poems*, ed. Daniel Jones (J.M. Dent & Sons, 1971)

Todd, Ruthven, *The Ghost of Dylan Thomas* (HappenStance, 2014)

Towns, Jeff, *Dylan Thomas: The Pubs*, illustrated by Wyn Thomas (Y Lolfa, 2013)

Watkins, Gwen, *Dylan Thomas: Portrait of a Friend* (Y Lolfa, 2005)

My own tributes to DT:

Under Milk Wood: An Illustrated Retelling by Cerys Matthews, illustrated by Kate Evans (Weidenfeld & Nicolson, 2022)

A Child's Christmas, Poems and Tiger Eggs—this oh-so festive story and some poems, set to music: Cerys Matthews and Mason Neely

Acknowledgements

Thank you, Pushkin Press, for the pleasure and opportunity of compiling this collection, to David Higham Associates and Dylan's family, Hannah and Trefor Ellis (who sang a mean Rev. Eli Jenkins at 4 a.m. in Swift's in New York), to those behind the superb collections I've loved over the years, edited by Walford Davies and Ralph Maud, and John Goodby, and Daniel Jones, to my Uncle Colin Edwards, and my family too for the laughs and love, and lastly to my most generous friend in Dylan Thomas, Jeff Towns, for providing invaluable assistance in gathering poems and images for this volume. My round's next.

Goodbye, but just for now.

AVAILABLE AND COMING SOON FROM PUSHKIN PRESS CLASSICS

The Pushkin Press Classics list brings you timeless storytelling by icons of literature. These titles represent the best of fiction and non-fiction, hand-picked from around the globe – from Russia to Japan, France to the Americas – boasting fresh selections, new translations and stylishly designed covers. Featuring some of the most widely acclaimed authors from across the ages, as well as compelling contemporary writers, these are the world's best stories – to be read and read again.

MURDER IN THE AGE OF ENLIGHTENMENT
RYŪNOSUKE AKUTAGAWA

THE BEAUTIES
ANTON CHEKHOV

LAND OF SMOKE
SARA GALLARDO

THE SPECTRE OF ALEXANDER WOLF
GAITO GAZDANOV

CLOUDS OVER PARIS
FELIX HARTLAUB

THE UNHAPPINESS OF BEING A SINGLE MAN
FRANZ KAFKA